Flirting with Mermaids

By the same author

Cape Horn to Starboard
Used Boat Notebook

Flirting with Mermaids

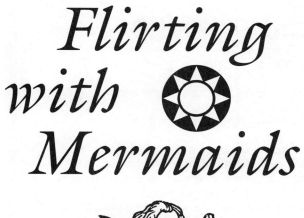

The Unpredictable Life of a Sailboat Delivery Skipper

JOHN KRETSCHMER

SHERIDAN HOUSE

First paperback edition published 2003 by
Sheridan House Inc.
145 Palisade Street
Dobbs Ferry, NY 10522

First published 1999 by Sheridan House Inc.

Library of Congress Cataloging-in-Publication Data

Kretschmer, John.
    Flirting with mermaids : the unpredictable life of a sailboat
delivery skipper / John Kretschmer.
        p.   cm.
        ISBN 1-57409-164-6 (alk. paper)
        1. Kretschmer, John—Journeys. 2. Voyages and travels.
3. Boats and boating. 4. Sailing. 5. Sailors—United States
—Biography. 6. Yachting. I. Title.
G440.K927K74 1999
910.4'5—dc21   98-47633
                                                                    CIP

Designed by Jeremiah B. Lighter

Printed in the United States of America

ISBN 1-57409-164-6

For Lesa, for understanding why I had to write
and for Joe, who will never sail the boat he built

Once I sat upon a promontory,
And heard a mermaid on a dolphin's back
Uttering such dulcet and harmonious breath
That the rude sea grew civil at her song
And certain stars shot madly from their spheres,
To hear the sea-maid's music.

WILLIAM SHAKESPEARE, A Midsummer Night's Dream

"Have you ever seen her?" he asked.
"Often and often."
"I, never."
"But have you heard her sing? How can she sing under the
water? Who could? She sometimes tries, but nothing comes
from her but great bubbles."
"She should climb on to the rock."
"How can she," he cried, quite angry. "The priests have
blessed the air, so she cannot breathe it, and blessed the rocks,
so that she cannot sit on them. But the sea no man can bless,
because it is too big, and always changing.
So she lives in the sea."

E. M. FORSTER, The Story of the Siren

"He had but little learning, except what he had picked up
from the sun and sea."

HERMAN MELVILLE, Moby Dick

Contents

Foreword

W HEN I FIRST met John Kretschmer he was flush with wanderlust. In those days, before the coming of GPS, he was wont to travel with his prized square wooden box that he'd clutch in his hands as if it were a crown jewel, as he walked it through the airport security checks. The box contained his sextant, which for John represented his life—his pride, spirit, love, joy, knowledge, and the world of water he plied—all in one.

It didn't happen overnight. John Kretschmer slipped into this life after a brush with fame after he doubled the Horn in possibly the smallest boat, a feat he achieved 15 years ago. If John had hoped to head off down a road of sailing fame, professional sailor *extraordinaire*, we know he would not have liked the regimen, the requirements, the business aspect of it. For, above all else, John Kretschmer represents one of the great free spirits of this world. When you read about his exploits you will begin to see him less as a yacht delivery captain and more as a person of amazing inner strength.

What I will always wonder about is how John Kretschmer has been able to keep his sense of humor. As things fall apart on all sides, while he dodges gunfire on the Arabian Sea, jumps into mid-ocean to wrap garbage bags around a leaking stern tube, mediates nasty crew problems, all while the weather gods are beating him to a pulp, there is always that slightly smart-aleck, sanguine person telling us in self-mocking tones how he managed to stay the course.

While John has spent 15 years sailing boats around the oceans of the world—some 200,000 miles, and more than 100 deliveries—he almost never turned back. We are surprised when he is forced to turn the unseaworthy ISOLETTA—as beguilingly beautiful that she was—back east, but not disappointed. It was one of the

rare times John Kretschmer was beaten by the mermaids, when
John would admit he kept that "romantic illusion" intact longer
than was in fact possible.

What is this life of the million waves that John Kretschmer has
ridden, where no one—but the mermaids—hears your whimpers,
hears you cry. "There are few professions . . . none that requires you
to extract this from yourself every minute of the day like yacht delivery," John says. And as you become a pawn of a world which you
have little control over, a little overconfidence and braggadocio on
the part of the captain can be overlooked as he, somehow, beyond
all misfortune, gets the boat to its destination. If that means sailing
the North Atlantic in January in a constant procession of gales, then
so be it. But it takes more than intensity and a lot of that lust for the
sea, and a sense of humor as strong as your will.

But deliveries are not all about danger. They are also about
persistent, impossible-to-remedy breakdowns that are constant and
about eking out miles, mile for mile, under ridiculous jury-rigged
arrangements as the only solutions. Deliveries are about dream
making, taking that boat to the arms of its loving owners on the
other side of oceans. And deliveries are about finding your way
through life, about being a guru, of sorts, to those "trying to catch
up with life," as John describes some of the passengers and crews
who sign aboard his deliveries.

It's impossible to know what the sea will throw at you, but it's
wonderful to live in its world, pulling from it a life that has no parallel. It is one where in the end, when you are alone out there, you
can begin to appreciate the mermaid gamboling off your bow, div-
ing under your keel, and through your life.

John Kretschmer knows a lot about mermaids. He might be a
world expert on them. That's what comes from a life at sea.

As you passage through these true sea stories, you will brush
with them, breathe the ocean world that John Kretschmer lives in,
and giggle at its fanciful nature.

Micca Leffingwell Hutchins
SAILING *Magazine*
August 1998

Flirting
with
Mermaids

Introduction

I discovered the ocean in my imagination
PETER FREUCHEN, Seven Seas

I MAKE LANDFALLS for a living. I sail other peoples' boats from one edge of an ocean to another and if I turn a deaf ear to the mermaid's song and the boat and I arrive as planned, I get paid, bid the crew farewell and saunter off into the sunset, or at least to the nearest bar.

My commitment may be three days, a week or several months; it is measured in nautical miles and always intense. There is mystery and a bit of foreboding in taking command of somebody else's boat, and pure magic in giving it back, complete with a list of suggested repairs.

Smug with the sense of accomplishment, feeling flush and free, I often tarry at my destination, reveling with the indulgence of hot water and sleep in intervals longer than four hours. I break out my notebook computer and dash off a piece for a sailing magazine. Then I search for a slant on a travel article, kick around plots for a novel and, while holed up in a small hotel room, puff out my chest and convince myself that, yes, with a lot of work, I could be the second coming of Ernest Hemingway—or at least old Joe Conrad—and maybe just publish another book someday. I should give up this crazy business of yacht deliveries and sailing schemes and just write for a living.

Soon the intoxication wears off. Writing is too damned much work and I begin to long for my real job. And then time works its magic and the inconveniences of the last passage are already forgotten. The leaks, the gales, the breakdowns, the quarrelsome crew: They fade away like a pale sunset. I am ready to go back to my waterfront office. I make my way to Fort Lauderdale, place a few phone calls, drop off my laundry, and before long I am clearing the inlet, punching into the easterly swell again.

Often my task is to coax somebody's old, forgotten dream boat across a large body of water. Then I will pass her on to a new innocent dreamer, brimming with visions of shimmering varnish, tradewind passages, tropical islands and fountains of youth. I connive to keep my customer's dreams intact, even if I have to lie like a politician when I turn the boat over at the end of a voyage. Dreams are private and fragile creations. We make them, live them or ignore them. Dreams are, however, as much a part of sailboats as teak planks and sistered oak frames, rusty steel plates, and the toxic chemicals that make up fiberglass mat, woven roving, and vinylester resin.

Keeping fantasies afloat is part of a sailboat delivery skipper's job description and you must be unusually sanguine by nature to survive in this business. And after enough time has passed, I tend to remember all the boats I have delivered to far-flung quay sides fondly—like old girl friends. Of course, there have been a lot of good boats. There was the powerful Ocean 71: running before a force too-much-blow in the North Sea, she never gave her crew an anxious moment. And there was the sleek Swan 41 that blasted around Cape Hatteras in a November snorter and the graceful Hylas 44 that meandered in and out of the eye of Hurricane Bob. Even the bad boats eventually find a soft spot in my mind's hard drive. That chubby French schooner had a terrible attitude and the 80-year-old Scottish pilot ketch did her best to sink out from under me. I should despise these boats—they tried to send me to a blue grave—but I don't. I accept them as part of the skipper's pact with Neptune. The ocean was never meant to be a place where you could cry for help. Besides, if I only delivered good boats, I wouldn't have enough material for a book.

More and more these days, I seem to be hired as one part skipper and one part guru. I dole out confidence and sage advice to new boat owners, who, despite the fact that they have a lot of money, fear that the truly important things in life, like offshore sailing and telling stories and bad jokes in seaside cantinas afterwards, are passing them by. My shipmates over the years, especially the owners, form an eclectic group: Americans sporting cowboy boots with Top-Sider soles, spurred on by quixotic quests; Europeans with skimpy Speedos, enchanting accents, and boats with a lot of right angles; and Japanese with too much money and all the right equipment. They also form a club of some my dearest friends and frequently remind me that riches are measured in many ways. If bluewater miles were traded as currency and sea stories had a par value, I'd be rubbing shoulders with Bill Gates.

Fortunately, I have reached a nice place in the evolutionary scale of skippers; I don't have to impress everybody I meet with my treasure trove of sailing knowledge anymore. All the while quietly keeping a keen eye on things, I can let others make their own discoveries. Delivering sailboats is probably the most over-rated, underpaid and, at times, exasperating job in the world. Yet, even after 15 years, more than 100 deliveries and nearly 200,000 miles, I still find it amazing that people pay me for doing what I love.

Sailboat delivery skipper was never an option at career day back in school. From the beginning, I knew I wasn't cut out for the routine of timely expectations; I resented the fact that my life was dictated by a clock. I could barely make it through a day of school. Not because I was inordinately stupid, I just couldn't take being confined in a classroom. I was born with a powerful wan-derlust. I don't know why but I have always insisted on steering my own course, a wayward course that invariably runs counter to conventional wisdom. Yet, I have managed to eke out a living doing the things that I love. One of my great accomplishments is that, to this day, I have never held a real job. If there is any advice, any lurking pearl of wisdom, hidden in this book, it's something as simple as how to go sailing at all cost while steering clear of the stealthy nine-to-five routine that slyly steals the only thing you own in life: your time. You may not want your sons and daughters to read any further.

They say rebels spring from the bottom of the family and I was the sixth of seven kids. Six of the seven were confirmed in the Lutheran church. At age 7, I told my mother that I was an atheist. She was surprised and slightly amused. I wasn't sure what an athe-ist was but I knew I didn't like church. Again, it was that sense of confinement that troubled me, especially that creepy thought that even if you were hiding, some omnipotent truant officer was keep-ing an eye on you. My tolerant and loving parents realized that no matter what they did, I was going to skip confirmation classes. They decided I would have to take my chances in life without the blessing of the church.

I was a mostly shy, indifferent student, but I had passion for the few subjects that intrigued me. By fifth grade I could name every English, French, Spanish and Portuguese mariner of note during the Age of Discovery. I didn't want to be a fireman, a policeman, an architect, an ophthalmologist, a malpractice lawyer or a copy-machine salesman. I wanted to be an explorer. My heroes were John Cabot, Jacques Cartier, Martin Frobisher, Francis Drake and, of course, the indomitable Ferdinand Magellan. I completely overlooked the inconvenient fact that my alter egos sailed with one hand on the tiller and the other on the cross. I assumed they had to go along with the religious mumbo jumbo of their sovereigns in order to obtain support for their voyages. However, like a juvenile version of the pirate in the Jimmy Buffett song, I had this vague notion that although I was only 10 years old, I had already been born too late. That was a depressing thought for a kid. But in the late 1960s, sailors weren't explorers anymore; that was the province of astronauts. Astronauts had to be good students. That didn't bode well for me. Then Francis Chichester came into my life.

I'll never forget the day when *Gypsy Moth Circles the World* turned up in the mail. My mother didn't realize what an impact something as facile as forgetting to return the card marked "please don't send this month's selection," would have on both of us. Although Chichester described his amazing solo circumnavigation in the crabby, crotchety prose of a bitter old man, I couldn't put the book down. I would read it in spurts, savoring it in my mind; it was the drug I never took. I never wanted it to end, and I even studied the boring appendices listing provisions and spare parts. I was amazed at how much corned beef that old bugger ate. I would stare at the picture of GYPSY MOTH screaming before the wind under staysail alone as she rounded Cape Horn. It was a revelation, something I never found in church: There were still adventures to be had for sailors. I dreamed that one day I would round Cape Horn in a small sailboat and write books about my sailing adventures. That Christmas I asked Santa for a sextant and an artificial horizon—unusual requests for a kid from Michigan who wasn't very good in math and had never been sailing.

But gradually, sailboats came into my life. First a Sunfish, which we sailed on a northern Michigan lake that was so cold you only capsized once, and then a few years later, a Sabre 28 sloop. My father had stunned us one Saturday morning by announcing that we were going down to the lake shore to buy a sailboat. We knew very little about sailboats and settled on the Sabre, which turned out to be a pretty good boat, simply because it had a pedestal and a wheel. I remember my father saying, "I'll be damned if I am going to spend 20,000 Dollars for a boat and steer it with a little stick." He didn't like the idea of a tiller which was a feature of the other boat we were considering, an Irwin 30. My two older brothers and I sailed OUR WAY almost every night of two summers on Lake St. Clair. Although we were usually plying shoal waters that most NBA power-forwards could stand in, we might as well have been in the Southern Ocean. We were enchanted by sailing, by the press of wind, by the natural elements that conspire to make a sailboat dance and a spirit soar. We taught ourselves to sail and were planning a grand expedition to the Lake Erie islands for the upcoming summer when my father's illness began to overtake him like a flood tide in the Bay of Fundy.

He had cancer in his lungs and in his bones. Dad, however, refused to submit to the deified preachings of his doctors. He would not die like one of their frogs in a jar of formaldehyde. He would not be drugged into a state of false hope, or radiated into a glowing shell, or buy meaningless time by subjecting himself to dehumanizing operations. He knew he was dying. He had worked too hard at living to die like a victim. He would die like a man, intact.

My father had a hard life. His parents were divorced, which was unusual in the 1930s, and he was raised by his father, an uncompromising Chicago cop. And those were days of cops and robbers. I have yellowed clippings from the *Chicago Tribune* describing how, more than once, brave officer Fred Kretschmer gunned down a bad guy on the street. Unfortunately, just as my father escaped the law and order of his machismo father's home, and went off to the University of Illinois, the war intervened. He joined the Army Air Force, as it was called then. He became a B-26 pilot, went first to North Africa and then to Europe, and somehow survived being shot down three times. After the war, he didn't want to fly anymore. He felt like he'd had his three strikes, that he was living on borrowed time, and after leaving the Air Force he struggled to support his ever-expanding family.

He had finally achieved some financial success when death came to his door. It didn't seem fair. He was only 53 and would not live to enjoy the fruits of his labors. But my father was not bitter. He'd had a great love affair with his wife, cherished his family, and had leaped enough hurdles. He was ready to die. He was just happy that at the end he had something to leave to his wife and kids. He wasn't haunted by the demons of regret; he could face death square in the eye. Dr. Kervorkian's clients aside, dying well as a virtue has gone out of fashion. But dying is life's last challenge. It is easier to die with dignity if you don't have to shoulder that heavy of burden of "If only I had done . . ."

My mother and I are kindred souls: We both look at the half-full cup of life with a good sense of humor, a fair bit of tolerance, just a few biases and many shared sailing adventures. On the other hand, my father and I were quiet companions. He passed away before we had a chance to really sail together, which, of course, is the only way to truly know someone. But the two of us often piled into the family car and drove for hours on end. Few words were spoken. There was a soft, "What do you say, John Rob?" a smile, a nod, an understanding and before long, another hundred miles of interstate highway disappeared beneath us.

I accompanied my father on many trips, both for business and out of curiosity, his and mine. As the forests and the meadows of the Midwest rolled by, I pictured myself exploring these lands for the first time. Whenever we came to water, I could feel my pulse quicken. Even if the water was just a muddy highway runoff, it didn't matter. Suddenly, I was aboard my ship, plying uncharted waters. My father, in silent fashion, reinforced my burgeoning wanderlust, never interrupting my reveries. He understood. Those long hours on the road served me well over the years, as I have always been able to cope with tedious passages.

I was 16 when it became obvious that my father was going to die, and I knew it was all my fault. I had made my pact with the devil long ago and now God was striking back at me. There is nothing as cold and numbing as a featureless hospital corridor in the cancer ward, death's waiting room, on a blustery January day in Detroit. It doesn't get any colder, any uglier. Any hint of optimism is buried beneath too many layers of gray to even ignite a search engine. It is a terrible time and a terrible place to die. It still gives me the shivers to think about it today, 22 years later. Death has its own schedule and Dad had the next appointment. One by one, we children were led into his room. By the time it was my turn, the visits were very short. I gave my father a kiss, tears raced down my cheeks and sobs wracked my chest. His body, once a powerful 200 pounds, was wasted, but his azure eyes still shined with life.

"Now don't cry, John Rob," he told me and actually managed a smile. "You are going to be the man around the house. Tom is on his own and Ed will be away at school. I am going to count on you to take care of your mom and little sister."

Then a stern-faced nurse led me out of the room. That was it. That was the last time I ever saw my father again. Those were the last stupid words I would hear him utter. I felt my childhood being ripped away from me. I didn't want to be the man around the house. I wanted my father back. I wanted to jump in the car and take a long drive, just the two of us. I wanted to laugh when we noticed familiar landmarks on I-75. I wanted to have lunch at a rest area on the Ohio Turnpike. I wanted to head down to Lake St. Clair and go sailing on OUR WAY.

When we returned home I went straight to my room and slammed the door behind me. Then I barricaded myself in the closet. Sitting in total darkness, I cried until my tear ducts turned into a desert. Eventually, I put my pride aside and tried to communicate with God. After a few busy signals, I got through. I didn't waste time with small talk or prayers. I offered him a solemn deal, a fair deal. I would start to believe, big time. In fact, I would even try to make up for lost time; I really would try. But, in the meantime, I needed a miracle; that was his business after all. That was the bargain. I realized I didn't have a lot of credit in God's bank and to ask for the loan of a miracle to save my father's life at this late hour was pretty audacious. But I was desperate and willing to put my very soul on the line.

I sat in the closet for a long time. It might have been three hours, maybe eight. I completely lost track of time, and space, too. I remember I peed in one of my shoes. I didn't know or care whether it was day or night. At some point, I came to accept that my father had died in that cold stone building on Eight Mile Road. He was gone. My credit application had been denied. Strangely, I wasn't filled with rage. I was completely spent. I felt a sense of serenity envelop me and then, later, I understood everything with a clarity I had never experienced before.

With my father's death, I realized that a part of me had died, too. The shy, indifferent part and the quiet and timid parts were gone. His passing had imparted a powerful sense of urgency into my existence. Life was something to be devoured because at any moment it might be snatched away. You just couldn't trust life. You had to seize life by the throat. You had to pursue your dreams relentlessly, recklessly. It was too much of a gamble to waste time. By the time I pushed open the closet door, I had put my affairs in order. I had even managed a working arrangement with God. I still wanted nothing to do with organized religion and mumbled dogmas but I acknowledged that a profound spirituality existed. We left it at that. I also knew that going to sea was no longer just a child's dream; it was my mission and there was no time to lose.

It may seem strange, or might be interpreted as stretching a metaphor, to claim that my father's death drove me out to sea. But from the perspective of 20 years and millions of waves later, I know that Dad's death hastened me along my watery way. It took a few years. I grazed in college, toying with the uncomfortable notion of preparing for a real job. I made a few feeble attempts to sustain my collegiate pole-vaulting career but my heart wasn't in it. I exorcised some demons by writing a terrible novel called *The Death of a Family*. Fortunately, I killed off the entire family by page 60 and couldn't think of anything else to say. By the time I was 21, I had a small boat and I was living on the ocean.

This is not a story about one person or one family going to sea in a boat and telling with the ballast of straight dope how you can do it too. This is a book about many different boats, in many different conditions, crewed by many different people. The common denominator is me. I calculated that I have sailed 30 different boats at least 1,000 miles a stretch and I have made well over 100 long-distance deliveries. Most so-called experts give you all the answers from the perspective of one or two boats; I'll show you how to make a muddle of things in a variety of boats, from 100-ton schooners, to shabby production boats, to ULDB sleds.

Like a fearless captain lemming, I have led hundreds of people over the cliff, introducing them to the wonders and horrors of offshore sailing. I don't have 10-point checklists or set-in-stone rules for better boat handling. I've learned to develop, hone and trust my instincts at sea—the essence of seamanship—and hopefully some of that spirit will come through in these pages. You might learn a technique or two from this book, but it is probably closer to a how-not-to than a how-to book.

On the surface, my job is deceptively simple: Take boat X from point A to point B, collect money and move along. Ah, but there are so many unpredictable dynamics at play, the foremost being a fiercely independent philosophy that permeates my soul. I have had many opportunities to slap Velcro epaulets on my shoulders and take a steady job, skippering a private luxury yacht and lurking around fancy marinas as if I owned them. I must admit that at times the prospect of a regular paycheck and a health insurance policy are alluring, but they run contrary to what I learned in the closet all those years ago. Sailing is certainly not a sport to me, or even a lifestyle. Sailing is my lifeline. Sliding across an ocean, propelled by spirit and sail, is synonymous with freedom. It is not freedom from responsibility, for sailboats are the most demanding of mistresses and nobody laughs at the concept of freedom like old Neptune. But my freedom is the ability to shake off the grip of society's expectations.

Although I am closing in on 40, I'm still more than willing to pit my wits against the guiles of the mermaid's song. I am an incorrigible flirt and too far offshore to turn back now. This is a book about conjuring sailing schemes and delivering sailboats, from world class yachts to barely afloat hulks, all over the world. It is a book about living a passionate, adventure-filled life on your own terms and accepting all the consequences of such a life. The only way I know how to write such a book is by a telling a few sea stories.

꿍꿍꿍꿍꿍꿍꿍꿍꿍꿍꿍꿍꿍꿍꿍꿍꿍꿍꿍꿍꿍꿍

CHAPTER 1

A
Shallow-Water
Appointment

Two courses, by the chart, now lay before us: the open sea (to Godthaab) and an inside passage between successive islands and the mainland. The outside course was much longer, and dirty weather was in prospect. That way, however, was my choice; and being then at the tiller I headed seawards.

ROCKWELL KENT, North by Northwest

IWAS LONGING FOR deep water, for blue water, for a dark passage beneath a canopy of stars without the burden of a landfall. I was the skipper of a cumbersome ketch plying the turquoise shallows behind the Belize reef. For a couple of months, we had reached west and north from the Bay Islands of Honduras, following an ancient trade route and racing the sun to the horizon each night.

Our ambitious project had taken us up jungle-lined rivers and through thundering reef passages. I am an offshore sailor at heart; I cross oceans to pay my bills. The shoal waters of the Western Caribbean had begun to unnerve me. I'd come to dread the gradual slowing and dull thud of fiberglass hitting sand and, worse, the sudden stop and angry grinding of fiberglass hitting coral. I longed for more than a foot or two between the short turtle grass and my bruised keel. I longed for a thousand fathoms of steely blue water beneath my bruised ego, and a destination on the other side of the world.

I had one more shallow-water appointment before heading

out to sea. I studied the runny pencil line on the coffee-stained sketch chart and, despite the fact that the fat centerboard ketch required six feet to float and the depthsounder recorded just seven feet of water, I made all speed toward a mangrove-bordered channel appropriately named Porto Stuck. I was hoping to catch the right side of high tide. Although there isn't much tide in Belize, six inches could make all the difference. I never imagined that six inches would change my life forever.

I had come to the steamy Caribbean coast of Central America on assignment for Sweden Public Television. I was the captain of an expedition doing research for a documentary film about the ancient Maya of the Yucatán Peninsula. We were examining the Maya in a fresh way, as mariners, and my Swedish partner had even concocted a fanciful theory that Mayan mariners were responsible for the mysterious collapse of their civilization more than a thousand years ago.

The project was the result of a crazy midwinter transatlantic yacht delivery, a blinding snowstorm, and several bottles of cheap Spanish table wine. It was February and I had just delivered an Ocean 71 from Newport, Rhode Island, to Stockholm, Sweden. (You'll read more about this wild winter ride in a later chapter.) Briefly, it is fair to say that the six-week voyage was brutal, as we were chased across the pond by a procession of westerly gales. I delivered the boat as scheduled and I was paid handsomely for my troubles. While in Stockholm, I called on my dear friend Christer Leferdahl. A planned short visit stretched into an all-night affair when we got buried by a sudden snowstorm. There was nothing to do but drink wine, and conjure up a scheme for a sailing project.

I first met Christer, a writer, artist and filmmaker, at the Café Sport in Horta on the beautiful isle of Faial in the Azores. Café Sport, locally known as Peter's, is run by the youngest Azevedo, José, who, as his father and grandfather before him, is a friend to all yachtsmen. Café Sport is a waypoint for transatlantic sailors—a legendary watering hole. We were both down on our luck. Christer, his lovely wife Annika and recently adopted Costa Rican son, were returning to Sweden after a two-year sailing sabbatical, and they were completely broke. They were without any cash until an errant funds transfer arrived because, in addition, their Visa card had just expired.

I was delivering a cranky schooner to France and my fuel-injection pump was the latest piece of equipment to expire. I bought Christer a drink and we bolstered each other's spirits. We started swapping sea stories and by the time Peter's pushed us out the door, I had agreed to loan Christer some money to get home. We stumbled back to the yacht harbor, arm in arm and singing what Christer assured me were bawdy Swedish sea chanteys.

A few years later, we were snug in front of a roaring fire, passionately discussing the regrettable way most historians view the oceans. Christer has an astonishingly wide swath of knowledge and the ability to sound like an expert on any subject, even in a language he doesn't like.

"Intellectuals are landblubbers," Christer insisted as he topped our glasses.

"That's lubbers, not blubbers," I said.

"Whatever. Historians view any expanse of water as a barrier and all but insurmountable to all pre-Columbian people."

Christer and I have a propensity for grand statements. I chimed in.

"The oceans weren't barriers. They were highways to discovery for ancient seafarers."

"Exactly," Christer agreed.

But before he could sneak in another word, I added, "Hell, Christer, I've sailed across the Atlantic 10 times and the Pacific twice. I know this doesn't say much for my chosen profession, but I am convinced that given adequate provisions and a stout piece of flotsam, just about anybody can cross an ocean during the right season."

This ridiculous statement made us both laugh and soon Annika was brewing a pot of coffee. Then Christer changed the subject.

"The film board wants me to do another project in Central America," Christer explained. "Do you have any ideas?"

Christer had recently completed a short documentary about the matriarchal society of the Kuna Indians of Panama's San Blas Islands. I began to think again about my recent passage to the Yucatán.

I have a keen interest in historical working vessels, and my far-flung yacht deliveries have given me the opportunity to examine and sail working boats from all over the world. Just before sailing to Sweden, I had delivered an old wooden ketch to Honduras. While in the Bay Islands, I became fascinated by the dugout canoes sailed offshore by local fishermen. These crude yet stout craft are little changed from the larger *cayucos* which the ancient Mayan mariners used to ply these same waters a thousand years earlier. I came to know a family of conch divers and learned to appreciate firsthand both the seaworthiness and tenderness of these simple boats.

My return flight from Honduras to Miami paralleled the Yucatán coast. The plane was almost empty and I jumped from window to window. The left side of the plane revealed dense jungle that covered the land like emerald paint. From the right side, I could see the Belize Reef, a natural sea wall, unbroken for hundreds of miles. The reef provided sheltered sailing for both north- and south-bound vessels. The plane finally veered offshore but somewhere over the Gulf Stream it dawned on me that it must have been a hell of a lot easier for the Maya to bridge their vast empire by water than by land.

"You should do a film about the Maya as mariners," I suggested and explained my embryonic theory.

Christer was intrigued. We fired up the computer and slapped together a hasty proposal for the film board. Eventually the coffee ran out, the snow stopped, and I made my way back to my tropical world. The film idea, like so many other great ideas, was filed away on Christer's hard drive.

Then a few months later Christer called and excitedly announced that the project was a go. How, I wondered, did he convince the film board to give him an advance for a research voyage?

"Oh, it was easy, John," he said with a laugh. "I told them that Mayan mariners were responsible for the collapse of classic Mayan civilization."

When I pressed him for details he just chuckled.

"Don't worry, I'll explain your theory when I see you. Now, can you meet me in Panama in about two weeks?"

"My theory?" I said, shocked.

"Yes," Christer said. "I told them that you were a famous captain and you had this crazy, but original, idea about the collapse of Maya civilization."

TALISMAN, a Heritage 46 ketch, designed by Charlie Morgan.

"Thanks, Christer. I'll see you in Panama."

Christer's 46-foot, Heritage ketch TALISMAN was lying at the dilapidated docks of the Panama Canal Yacht Club in Colón on the Caribbean side of the canal. When I arrived, laden with spare parts, Christer and Stephen, the expedition cook, were barely on speaking terms.

"He's driving me nuts," Christer complained, using his best American slang. "He's the cook but he wants to eat out every night. We've been here a week and he still hasn't learned how to light the stove. At this rate I'll be out of money before we reach Guatemala and he won't have prepared a single meal."

Christer began to grumble about the rain and I realized that we needed to get moving fast or our grand project might bog down in dreary Colón. I went to work immediately, rebuilding the hydraulic steering system. I worked through the night. By morning, although the system was held together by a combination of hose clamps and good faith, I pronounced it fit and told Christer to clear customs.

When Christer returned to the boat he was more depressed than before. As so often happens in a foreign country, he had lost track of the date. That rainy Thursday in early October, our departure day, was a religious holiday in Panama and all official offices were closed.

"I even tried bribes," Christer said exasperated.

Knowing Christer, they were not substantial bribes.

"Relax, Christer," I said quietly. "It's only a short delay. It will give us another day to get the boat ready."

Christer looked at me forlornly. "John, tomorrow is Friday. We can't leave. It's bad luck."

With that statement, Stephen, who had seemed quite pleased at the prospect of getting underway and was actually in the throes of preparing breakfast, threw his hands up in the air and stormed into his cabin.

While superstition is for the ignorant, the uninformed, the kind of people who consult their astrologer before investing in pork bellies or proposing marriage, I must admit there is something to this leaving-port-on-Friday business. I know it's just an arbitrary name for the sixth day of the week, conceived by some landlubbing medieval German chap who worshipped Freya, the goddess of love, and has no nautical significance whatsoever. But I sympathized with Christer. I remember once clearing Bermuda on a Friday. We were bound for Cape Horn but only three days later, we had capsized in a violent gale. On a delivery to Japan, I cleared Fort Lauderdale on a Friday and a few days later we were riding through the eye of Hurricane Floyd. Friday stories could go on and on; I knew we had to get under way. It was better to risk the wrath of the gods than spend another day in Colón.

We obtained clearance early the next morning and a waxen sun even made an appearance before quickly disappearing into the dawning gloom. Within an hour, the massive stone jetties protecting the outer harbor disappeared astern, falling off the edge of the world as the sky, horizon and water merged into a gray conspiracy. We were bound for the island of Guanaja, 700 miles away off the coast of Honduras.

It was our first night out. I had come on deck at 2200, relieving Stephen of his watch, only to find that TALISMAN was headed back toward Panama. The autopilot had taken the night off, the boat had quietly gybed and Stephen, who was absorbed scribbling in his journal, hadn't noticed. I didn't scream at him. I waited till he was in his bunk before I turned the boat around and back on course. Stephen was an intriguing shipmate. A former Stockholm lawyer turned hotel operator and struggling artist, Stephen had one passion in life. Every year he made a pilgrimage to Pamplona to run with the bulls.

He had attended one of Christer's lectures where he learned about our expedition and then pestered Christer until he agreed to take him along. Stephen turned up at the airport with two massive, brimming suitcases. His basic travel kit included ornate brass candlestick holders to provide the right atmosphere for the elegant dinners he promised to prepare, several elaborately embroidered tablecloths, and a 17th century Japanese smoking jacket, among other items.

We made our way north, skirting the numerous shoals and off-shore banks that lay like a minefield off the coast of Nicaragua. We were about 50 miles off Cabo Gracias a Dios (Cape Thank God) as Christer sat back and explained to me my brilliant theory of how mariners caused the collapse of classic Mayan civilization.

"You see, John, as the Maya developed bigger and more seaworthy canoes, the ease of marine transportation diminished the social importance of the mighty inland cities which led to their abandonment."

I rolled my eyes. The Maya created North America's first advanced civilization. The classic period began a few hundred years after the birth of Christ and flourished for nearly a thousand years. Their realm was the Yucatán Peninsula, which juts off Mexico like a left thumb. From misty highlands in the south, to central swamps, to dry scrub in the north, the Maya hewed their civilization from a harsh land. Long-distance trade was vital and scholars now concede that maritime commerce played an important role in linking the extremes of their empire. However, sometime around 800 A.D., the Maya civilization collapsed. Great cities like Tikal and Copán were mysteriously abandoned. Nobody can say for sure what caused the breakdown but dozens of theories, ranging from severe droughts to abduction by space beings, have been postulated by a host of scholars, amateurs, mystics and lunatics. We were the first, however, to propose that it was actually a bunch of sailors that caused all the trouble.

"That's it?" I asked laughing. "That's all it took to get the money?"

"No, let me explain," Christer said, trying to be serious. "You know that Mayan priests and shaman wielded absolute power and didn't hesitate to offer up human sacrifices to appease the gods. Well, these priests used certain precious, pious items like manatee bones, quetzal feathers and conch shells to communicate with the gods. However, when low-level priests in obscure coastal villages were able to obtain these same religious objects from marine traders, it undermined the entire ceremonial structure of the priesthood. Simply put, the people on the street no longer believed the priests to be divine and decided that it was more prudent to leave town rather than risk being called on to do their civic duty and meet Itzamná, Ix Chel and other gods and goddesses personally."

Just as Christer finished with his or, I should say, my wacky-yet-plausible theory, a wave crashed over the stern, flooding the cockpit. We were sailing on a lovely broad reach and while the easterly tradewind was brisk, it certainly wasn't strong enough to spawn waves capable of pooping TALISMAN. What was going on? Were we sailing over an uncharted bank? We suddenly realized that

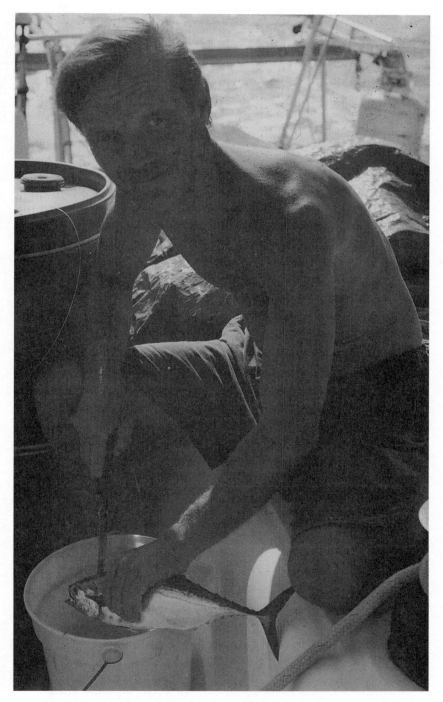

My friend and associate, Christer Leferdahl.

we were dead in the water. The sails were billowing with air but we were not moving. We couldn't be aground. The water wasn't deep but there were at least 20 fathoms below the keel. Then Christer figured out we had probably snagged a lobster pot with our prop.

Christer and I dashed below. The strain on the prop and shaft was tremendous and the boat shuddered with each wave. I feared we might pull the 1½-inch stainless steel shaft right out of the boat, which would not be a good turn of events, and hollered for Stephen to lower all sail. We tried to rotate the shaft by hand but it was completely wrapped and impossible to move. There was only one thing to do. I donned mask and fins and, armed with a sharp knife, plunged over the side.

There is something creepy about swimming 50 miles offshore and something dangerous about trying to free a prop wrap from a 20-ton boat bucking around like a spastic blue whale in 8- to 10-foot seas. I made several attempts to cut the thick nylon cord, only to retreat just before being walloped by the plunging stern. I needed tension on the cord and screamed for Christer and Stephen to unroll the genoa. Struggling to tread water, I made one more dive to cut the cable, which was now taut, when suddenly it parted on its own. We were free. Unfortunately, within seconds TALISMAN seemed like she was a mile away. Struggling to stay afloat, I wondered why I hadn't put on a life jacket. I tried not to think about Christer and Stephen arguing about what was the best method of coming back to rescue me as the boat charged on toward Honduras. Finally, TALISMAN started back in my direction. As I waited for my ship to come in, I concluded that Ix Chel, the Mayan goddess of fertility and seafarers—a strange combination to be sure but one that would have significance for me soon enough—didn't buy our theory.

We eventually raised the verdant island of Guanaja and after a short stay pressed on for Guatemala's sweet river, the Rio Dulce. We had plotted a route to follow the watery trade route of obsidian, a volcanic glass found in the highlands of Guatemala. Obsidian, which can be honed into a blade edge sharper than surgical steel, was an important tool used, among other things, to rip out the hearts of those unlucky volunteers off to meet the gods. Once it reached the coast, obsidian was loaded aboard ocean-going dugout canoes and traded up and down the Yucatán Peninsula. Obsidian chips and objects found on remote offshore cays are the prime bits of evidence confirming that the Maya had extensive waterborne commerce. One of the focal points of this lively commerce, according to early Spanish records, was the port city of Nito.

Although repeated professional archaeological expeditions have failed to find any remains of Nito, which is believed to have been situated near the mouth of Rio Dulce, Christer and I decided we would poke around anyway. After a wild night at the disco in Livingston, a Garifuna village on the other side of the river, we piled into my sea kayak and paddled toward the far bank. As we drew near the swampy shoreline, I remembered the disturbing advice of a young woman I'd danced with the night before.

Straining to be heard over blown-out speakers blaring out a weird combination of marimba and Marley, she told me that her mama still went to the house of spirits every afternoon. I knew that the Garifuna, descendants of native Caribes and escaped slaves, practiced a form of voodoo and communicated with spirits. I wondered if her mama knew anything about the location of Nito. When I asked about Nito, she looked terrified.

"What's the matter? Does Nito have something to do with the gods or spirits?"

Something about the disco, the swaying, sweating, scantily clad, black bodies, the dirt floor, purple lights and pulsing music made me feel dizzy, and suddenly nervous.

"Hell no," she said laughing, breaking my spell. "It ain't got nothin' to do with no gods, it's the tommy gobbers."

"The what?"

"The tommy gobbers, you know, yellow jaws, snakes man, mean mother snakes, bite you ass for fun. They ain't no Nito over there but they be tommy gobbers. You watch out for them tommy gobbers too because they don't bite no Indians but they like black and white."

I made the mistake of telling Christer about the tommy gobbers and, typically, he knew all about them. He informed me that the snake was usually called a *fer-de-lance* and did, indeed, have a nasty reputation.

"I believe it has the largest fangs of any poisonous snake," he said clinically, adding, "and it has a bad attitude. It has been known to chase people when disturbed."

We spent a couple of hours combing the coastline, examining rocks and shells, swatting at the aptly named no-see-ums and, for me at least, trying not to think about, and more importantly, not to disturb, any tommy gobbers. We found absolutely no signs that a once-great port city had occupied this muddy riverbank 1,000 years ago. Christer overheard my sigh of relief as we climbed into the kayak and paddled back to the boat.

"Were you really worried about the snakes?" he asked teasingly.

"Of course not," I lied, wiping the sweat from my brow.

We steered TALISMAN toward Belize, guided by the seven hills of Punta Gorda, a natural landmark on the western horizon. Chasing history, especially nautical history, is always fraught with risk. As we made our way along the coast of Belize, we tarried at several coastal sites and examined small piles of rocks with strained enthusiasm. While it is easy to be stirred by brooding pyramids rising mysteriously from dark jungles, silent canoes leave no footprints, no record of their passing along the protean surface of the sea. Still, with persistence and imagination, we made a few quiet discoveries.

We found obsidian chips and potsherds on remote offshore cays. Actually, we didn't find them; Stephen did. We had picked up another crew member at Livingston, my friend Tim Budziak, a dentist craving adventure. While Christer, Tim and I would painstakingly comb a pebbly beach, Stephen would stroll around and announce, "This is interesting," as he effortlessly reached down and picked up one shiny piece of obsidian after another. We sailed *cayucos* with conch fishermen and swam with manatees in a dark lagoon while visiting a rustic fish camp. We spent many days living with a Maya family in a coastal village. Most importantly, we came to know something of the sailing conditions the Maya had mastered centuries before. We managed to piece together an outline and script and by the time Christer and Tim left the boat in Belize City, we felt that we had enough material to make a film.

Not shackled by any annoying real-world responsibilities like a job or family to return to, I volunteered to continue on. We wanted to examine a few coastal sites in northern Belize before clearing the reef and sailing offshore for Mexico, where we planned to leave the boat for the winter. Stephen remained behind with me.

With the southeast wind building, we neared the rusty tripod and crooked fishing stakes marking the channel at Porto Stuck.

"Okay, Stephen, hold on." Although our timing was perfect, an hour before high tide, I held out little hope that we would make it through the quarter-mile gap between two scrubby mangrove cays. Stephen, completing a sketch in his journal, seemed unconcerned. He had a lot of confidence in my navigation despite the fact that, at last count, I had put us aground 12 times, and looked at me as if to say, "It's in Ix Chel's hands now, so why worry about it."

Maintaining speed so that we might bounce over any hidden shoals, I held the wheel firmly, my knees braced, ready for impact. But Ix Chel smiled on us at last, indeed. I could never have known what grand plans that devious goddess had in store for me, as I cleaned the sweat from my sunglasses and realized that we had cleared the channel.

After a brief stop at Cay Caulker and a futile search for suspected burial mounds, we sailed on to Ambergris Cay, the only real tourist center in Belize. Our plan was simple: We wanted a nice meal ashore in a restaurant with something other than rice and beans on the menu, a few cold beers, and a good night's sleep. At first light, we would clear the reef and make our way north in deep water, glorious deep water.

The best thing about sandy streets is that they absorb rain, they don't make puddles, and you don't need elaborate drainage systems. Stephen and I walked up Front Street in a persistent drizzle. The rainy season, refusing to yield, had stretched well into December. San Pedro, the main community on Ambergris Cay, lined with small hotels and funky bars, is surprisingly charming. The community caters mostly to scuba divers from the States. Divers are undemanding travelers. As long as the water is clean, the reef is alive, and the fish abundant, they will put up with just about anything on the surface. I am always amazed when I eavesdrop on divers discussing their travels. They could be comparing exotic locales like the Sinai Peninsula in the Red Sea, the islands of the Great Barrier Reef, Fiji and the Seychelles, yet all they talk about is whether the coral was soft or hard and how many damned fish they saw. They never talk about the people, the politics, the geography or any of that other insignificant stuff that you can observe while breathing naturally without 50 pounds of gear on your back.

We had nearly covered the entire six blocks of Front Street when we ducked into Fidos to get out of the rain. The beachfront bar, covered by a leaking palapa, was empty except for a lovely blond lady. She was perched on a stool in the corner of the bar, writing postcards and drinking a Beliken, the local beer. Stephen, a dapper fellow by nature, who I thought looked a bit ridiculous dressed in a fancy silk shirt in soggy San Pedro, hurried over to her and politely asked permission to sit down. I trailed behind. She looked up and smiled, her perfect white teeth accentuated her sunburned face.

"Sure." she said. "This is about the only dry place on the island. All it does is rain here, so my advice to you guys is to sit down and drink heavily."

We took her advice. Lesa, pronounced like Lisa, had been traveling in Mexico and Belize for several months, looking for a place to put down stakes and set up a business. Just 29 (or so she said, but I believed her because she looked about 25) and traveling alone, she had been a successful computer broker in Santa Cruz, California, before becoming disenchanted with the material madness of fast-track sales. The tragic death of her father a few months before had pushed her over the edge, and she set off for points south. She had enough money stashed to spend a year traveling around Central America before deciding where to set up shop, whatever that shop might be.

"I have several ideas, in fact I have a whole list of ideas," she said laughing as she pulled out a notebook from her handbag labeled 'Business Ideas'. "It will probably be a tourism business of some kind, but I know it won't be in San Pedro."

"Why not?" I asked.

"It's too small. I've been here three weeks and I know everybody already. Most businesses are run by gringos who spend all day getting drunk and complaining that things aren't as they used to be. If one more person tells me I should have been here 10 years ago, I'll strangle him."

I was intrigued by Lesa. She didn't fit into the usual categories defining Americans south of the border. She wasn't a hippy wannabe, hopping along the so-called gringo trail, looking for cheap pot, meaningful cultural experiences (which usually meant trying to sleep with the locals, a task much easier for *las gringas*) and hefting her belongings on her back like a crooked mule. She wasn't the Texas type either, looking to take Central America by storm with good old-fashioned American capitalism and bullshit. And she wasn't in some midlife crisis. She was definitely still on the right side of mid, with no obvious crisis on her sleeve.

Was she running from a love gone astray? She certainly didn't seem downtrodden. She oozed with confidence, even though she had no concrete plans. She'd had some experience in life that was obvious and she had a terrific sense of humor. She was also beautiful, and sparks were flying. Poor Stephen had to move out of the way or risk being burned. A true gentleman, he excused himself and suggested that I take his stool. Never much of a gentleman, I accepted.

"What are you doing here?" Lesa asked. "You don't look like a tourist."

"Is that good that I don't look like a tourist?" I asked and thought to myself, maybe I should have shaved. Or maybe it is my moldy foulweather gear, not typical tourist garb.

Lesa smiled, "That depends. What do you do?"

"I am a writer and a sailboat captain. I deliver sailboats all over the world."

Let's face it, that is a great line in a bar. I could see Lesa's eyes light up and that was a nice sight to see. Later I heard a Belizean customs official tell her that her eyes were a shade of blue that belonged in a museum. That is also a great line in a bar.

I explained our film project, making it sound much more impressive than it was, and invited Lesa to dinner. I told her that we were looking for a nice place and she suggested a small Italian café. An Italian restaurant in Belize sounded suspect. But I had come to know and appreciate the anomalies that defined this beautiful, mixed-up, English-speaking little country which sometimes seems more like a Caribbean island or a West African republic than a part of Central America. The Italian restaurant would probably serve rice and beans with a ketchup red sauce, but in Belize that would seem right.

Surprisingly, we had a lovely Italian meal, complete with several bottles of Chianti. I was falling in lust. Lesa was designed just the way I think a woman should be. She was tall and lean with broad shoulders and a firm, nicely proportioned, athletic body. Her blond hair was streaked from the sun and fell down to her shoulders in waves. Dressed in a tank top, denim shorts and flip-flops, she seemed at ease in the tropics. But I surmised that if she wanted, she could also look elegant.

"Where are you headed next?" I asked, with a cunning ulterior motive running around in my brain.

"Either Antigua, in Guatemala, to learn Spanish, or maybe back to Cozumel. I really liked Cozumel."

"Did you know that Cozumel was the home of Ix Chel, the Maya patron saint of sailors?" I left out the fertility goddess part, thinking that might be a bit too suggestive.

"Really," Lesa said, not particularly impressed.

"Well, that's where we are going. We're leaving tomorrow. How would you like to sail with us and pay your respects to Ix Chel? Traveling by sea is the only way to go to Cozumel."

Lesa smiled, revealing those whitest of teeth (I've always been a sucker for a nice smile) and said, "I haven't done much sailing. How long will it take to get there?"

"Oh, not long." I lied. "It's just less than 200 miles and we have a strong, favorable current. Less than a day for sure."

I neglected to mention that the sketchy forecast I had picked up in a dive shop called for stiff northerly winds which would make the passage less than pleasant.

"That sounds like fun," Lesa said. "But there is one problem. I had a few boxes of household items shipped down here. You see, I thought I was going to make San Pedro my base, but I have changed my mind. I'll have to do something with my stuff."

"That's not a problem," I assured her. "The boat is big. There is plenty of room for your gear; we'll just stow it aboard. Believe me, it will be much easier to clear your stuff through customs on a boat than at a border crossing ashore."

"Are you sure there will be room?"

"I'm positive. I mean how much stuff can you have? I'll meet you in front of your hotel at 0700 tomorrow."

To this day I am not sure whether Lesa was more excited about sailing with me or at the prospect of having someone help move her gear. As I walked up Front Street the next morning, I was convinced that she would have come to her senses during the night and would be nowhere to be found on this drizzly morning. I felt a pang of regret. I was sure I wouldn't see her again, just another chance encounter of a traveling man that lead nowhere. But to my surprise and delight, there she was, smiling and waving, and there were her boxes. Five enormous boxes.

Resisting the urge to say, "What in the hell do you have in those boxes?" I smiled wanly and said, "You do have a quite a bit of stuff, good thing you're not traveling by backpack."

Lesa shrugged her shoulders. She was obviously embarrassed. "As I said, I was planning to set up housekeeping here."

She must have lived in a mansion in California, I thought to myself, and inadvertently whistled. "I think we'll have to hire the water taxi to load them on the boat, but that's okay." I added cheerfully, "We'll manage."

"Welcome aboard TALISMAN." Stephen, dressed in a resplendent kimono, greeted Lesa with a cup of tea after we hefted the last of her boxes aboard and crammed them down the companionway.

He was delighted to have, as he put it, "some female company aboard," and I think pleased that someone else had as much stuff as he did.

Designed by Charley Morgan, TALISMAN was absolutely cavernous below. Love him or loathe him, Charley, a friend of mine, has designed more diverse sailboats than any designer. I have sailed 60-footers that did not have as much room as TALISMAN. The secret was simple: She carried her colossal beam a long way forward and aft.

Needless to say, she did not perform all that well, especially sailing to weather. In fact, if the wind was much forward of the beam, she lumbered along like a seasick manatee, doing battle with the ocean, desperately trying to push the water out of her way instead of gliding over it or at least crashing through it. And, unless the centerboard was down, she made appalling leeway. She was, however, robustly constructed, and I liked her.

Unfortunately, the forecast was accurate and a blustery north wind, a direct head wind, greeted us as we cleared the dog-legged channel through the reef. Right from the start, it was rough sailing as TALISMAN and the ocean went after each other. The powerful north-setting current collided with the strong, contrary wind to create lumpy seas. I was afraid Lesa would be seasick. I should not have worried. She took to sailing immediately and whooped with joy as we crashed into steep waves. Stephen, on the other hand, wasn't feeling well at all. The best remedy for seasickness is to take your mind off it, so I put him on the helm.

Lesa and I went forward to greet a pod of gamboling dolphins. They skidded by the bow one after another while we clutched the pulpit and cheered them on.

"We're just about at the Belize-Mexico border," I said to Lesa, gazing at the fast fading coastline.

"Where is the dotted line?" she joked.

"Are you okay?" I asked. "It is getting pretty rough out here."

"I'm fine."

I was falling in love. I mean this woman was not only beautiful and seemingly fearless, she didn't get seasick either!

By early afternoon, the wind began to howl, triggering a frightful moan from the partially furled mainsail. A full-blown norther was taking shape and I knew that the conditions would be ugly by nightfall. I studied the chart and decided to head for Xcalak, a tiny Mexican port of entry just north of the border. The pass through the reef was narrow, just a couple of boatlengths across. I swallowed hard, winked at Lesa, and began our approach. White water was crashing on both sides of the reef making it nearly impossible to spot the opening. I sheeted the mainsail flat and put the engine in gear to maintain speed and keep the boat from rolling too much with the stiff beam-on sea. I prayed that the heading given in the guidebook was accurate. Reef running requires commitment. Once in the pass, there is no backing out. With my eyes darting nervously from the reef to the depthsounder, we shot into the harbor. Although my heart was pounding, I smiled casually at Lesa and said quietly, "There's nothing to it."

The harbor shoaled rapidly and we had to get the anchor down quickly. I dashed forward while Stephen took the helm. I kicked our big plow over the side but it just skipped along on a hard bottom of thin sand and rock. Our windlass was not operational and three times I manhandled the 60-pound anchor and ⅜-inch chain back aboard. I was exhausted but we had to get the anchor to bite or head back out to sea. Finally, I donned my familiar mask and snorkel and, once again, plunged overboard. Lesa dropped the anchor as Stephen steered the boat into the wind. I frantically dug the plow head into the bottom. It finally set. I struggled to the surface gasping for air, hauled myself aboard, and collapsed into the cockpit.

"Is that the normal way of setting an anchor?" Lesa asked, seriously.

Stephen answered, with a perfectly straight face, "Why, of course."

After we were certain that the anchor was indeed holding, we went ashore for dinner. Unfortunately, the outboard engine on our small Whaler dinghy had also quit working and we had to paddle. With the stiff breeze behind us, we flew ashore. The guidebook describes Xcalak as a "sleepy village at the end of a long dirt road." That pretty well sums up the place. There is no need to waste adjectives on Xcalak. After clearing customs, we went in search of dinner. The only place in town was a dirty little cantina filled with flies and drunks. Several patrons were passed out face down on the tables and most of the others were steering a course to the same destination. This explained why, in an otherwise sleepy village, the only neon sign belonged to the "AA" building. Trying to ignore the ubiquitous cockroaches, we choked down some pretty good *pescado con ajo* and a few Dos XXs before making our way back to the dinghy.

Although TALISMAN was just a couple hundred yards off the beach, it took us an hour to reach her. Have you ever tried paddling a Boston Whaler skiff into a 30-knot breeze with clumsy and heavy mahogany paddles designed specifically for a sixth-century *cayuco*? It's virtually impossible but, sadly, these were the only paddles we had for the dinghy. At first Stephen and I paddled side by side but after 20 minutes we had hardly moved. Then I moved to the bow and propped on my knees, began stroking like a wild man, first on one side, then on the other. Inch by inch, we crawled toward the boat. Lesa sat in the middle and bailed frantically. But it was no use; the dinghy was essentially under water. Stephen was a sight to behold. Once again, he had donned his fancy silks for our shoreside excursion, this time black shorts and shirt highlighted by a magnificent red bandanna in his hair. Sitting high, and only a little drier, in the stern, he paddled slowly but steadily, while offering me technical advice.

"John, John, please, only on the left. One of my strokes is

equal to two of yours and we are out of balance when you paddle so aggressively."

I was tempted to reach back and whack him with my 50-pound log of mahogany masquerading as a paddle. Finally, we reached TALISMAN's stern ladder and threw ourselves aboard. Climbing over the rail, Stephen wiped salt from his eyes and, while hanging his bandanna in the rig to dry, remarked casually, "Well, that was a bit of a struggle, wasn't it?"

We remained in Xcalak the next day, pinned down by the wind and confined to the boat. It didn't matter. Lesa and I were falling madly in love. We'd only known each other a couple of days but there was magic between us. She was fascinated by TALISMAN and, for the first time, considered cruising by sailboat as both a means of travel and a lifestyle. I was fascinated by her. We talked about the many boats I have sailed, the many places they have carried me to, and the many places I still wanted to explore. We talked about sailing off together. Our discussions were broad and general, the best kind of discussions for falling in love. There were no plans made but a rough framework was being sketched out. The wind finally eased up that night and we made our way through the pass and north to Cozumel.

In Cozumel we secured the boat at the Club Náutico and Lesa and I checked into a small beachfront hotel. Stephen invited us to an elaborate farewell dinner only to remember when the bill arrived that he had no money. The next morning he caught a flight for the mainland. He was homeward bound for Sweden. I couldn't help but laugh as I watched him bound up the ramp. Throughout the voyage he had collected local clothing and as he turned and waved, he looked like a reincarnation of Kukulcan. It wasn't difficult to picture Stephen, completely draped in Mayan garb, as the mysterious great white god that haunts Maya legends. In spite of the fact that he owed me a rather hefty sum of money that I knew I would never see, I was sad to see my eccentric shipmate leave.

Lesa and I spent a couple of lovely days in the sun. We rented a Jeep and explored the ruins of San Gervasio, the home of my friend Ix Chel. As we picked our way through fallen rocks, Lesa confided to me that she had to leave soon for Cancún. By previous arrangement, she was meeting a friend. Since she had already paid for his ticket, she had better be there to meet him. Two days be-

Stephen, a Swedish artist and the expedition cook, riding the bow wave.

fore Christmas, it had been a strange afternoon of laughing and crying until Lesa boarded the ferry for Cancún, and I set sail alone for Isla Mujeres. But I knew I'd see her again. I had to, I had her boxes.

CHAPTER 2

A Show
of Presence

*I felt as if everything bad in my life had remained onshore
and everything good was out on the water with me. We went
below, shared a can of tuna fish with saltines and drank
warm beer. On the quilt-covered bunk we lay in each other's
arms until morning, whispering.*

BOB SHACOCHIS, Dead Reckoning

WE WERE GATHERED in front of the frightening life-sized television set, with grunts and groans ricocheting off the walls, watching another football game when the phone rang.

"It's her," my brother-in-law informed me with a smirk and plopped back into his recliner to see if the Dolphins scored on third and goal.

I was relieved to be released from the Christmas Day ritual of stuffing yourself full of food and then retiring to the nearest padded room to watch an endless parade of football games. After another hiatus without television, the relentless commercial interruptions seemed more annoying than usual. I felt strangely disconnected from the shameless pitching of products, America's electronic version of Third World street hawkers, and suddenly remembered why I hadn't spent many holidays at home recently. During a decade and a half of wandering, I have managed to miss Christmas regularly. I'd much rather spend time with my family at another time of year, without the pressure of frantically trying to buy trinkets that nobody needs.

After sailing all night, I left TALISMAN in the capable hands of

Manuel Gutierrez, my friend and the owner of Marina Paraiso in Isla Mujeres and flew back to Florida. Having just spent three months drifting about Central America, the suburbs of Fort Lauderdale seemed foreign and a little daunting as I made my way to my sister's house for Christmas dinner. Although I have made Fort Lauderdale my base for years, I almost never venture west of I-95 where ocean-access canals dry up and reams of insatiable subdivisions with snappy, pseudo-Spanish names, intent on swallowing up what's left of the Everglades, begin. I'm convinced that one of these days when I come back after a delivery, Fort Lauderdale and Naples, on the Gulf coast, will be joined, probably by an air-conditioned drive-through outlet mall.

At halftime I excitedly confided to my sister that I had fallen in love in Mexico. Terri is a romantic like me and was thrilled with my news, but my dear friend Dick, her stoic husband with a wonderful sardonic humor, was skeptical of whirlwind romances in far-off lands.

"I doubt you'll hear from her again," he informed me knowingly. "Besides," he continued, "she has a tattoo. What kind of girl has a tattoo?"

I didn't realize that the small shark and dolphin emblazoned on Lesa's right shoulder would have such an impact on my proper brother-in-law. Or maybe I did. That is probably why I described it in such detail. He was particularly worried about the good-versus-evil symbolism of the tattoo and didn't buy Lesa's view of the dolphin and shark as some sort of yin-yang connection.

"Her" meant Lesa. I sprang to my feet, winked at my brother-in-law, and took the call in the privacy of the bedroom.

"Hello."

"Hello."

"Where are you? This can't be a Mexican phone connection. You sound like you're right next door."

"Unfortunately, I'm still in Cancún, standing at a pay phone in the rain."

"How is it going?" I asked, dying to know but not quite sure how to say "with him," the mysterious old boyfriend from California who was visiting.

I was hoping that it was not going well. So instead I babbled, "It's still raining down there, that's a shame. It's beautiful here in Fort Lauderdale, sunny, warm."

What an idiot, I thought to myself. I've been home one day and I already sound like an announcer on the Weather Channel.

"Yes, it is still raining," Lesa said calmly, "but somehow the rain isn't as tolerable without you."

My heart raced. So it wasn't going well.

"I have a suggestion," she continued. "Why don't I come to Florida for New Year's Eve and we'll start the year off right?"

"That is a great idea," I said out loud, trying to remain calm and controlled while pumping my fist and silently mouthing, "Yes! Yes! Yes!"

"Oh, there is one more thing," Lesa said. "Do you mind if I leave my boxes on the boat? I'll figure out what I am going to do with all that stuff when I get back."

"Of course, I don't mind, *no problema, amiga.*"

"Great. Then I'll call you in a couple of days with my travel plans. *Hasta luego* and Merry Christmas."

"*Feliz Navidad.*"

My excitement was slightly tempered by the inconvenient prospect of quickly explaining the situation to my current girlfriend. I decided to go with the truth, reasoning that it would find its way to the surface soon enough and would ultimately be less painful. Besides, after a three-month separation, I didn't think there was much umph left to our affair anyway. The day after Christmas I drove to her apartment. I should have lied. I came bearing gifts from Guatemala, hoping to soften the blow, but they didn't have the desired effect. In the end, I was lucky to survive as I hastily retreated through the back door amid a barrage of flying ceramic turtle masks and brightly colored maracas.

Lesa arrived at the madhouse Miami airport a couple of days later. As I stood nervously waiting for her to clear customs, I suddenly panicked. Would I remember what she looked like? We'd spent a mere week together. What if I didn't recognize her, how embarrassing. Of course, I'd remember her. I'd spent every second of seven days with her. There she was in the crowd, tall, tan and graceful. She was smiling at me with those lovely teeth and was soon smothered in my arms. My hunch had been right; she could look elegant. I whisked her home to my flat on the Intracoastal Waterway in Fort Lauderdale and soon became intimately reacquainted with why I was so smitten with this woman. We ate smoked salmon, drank a couple of bottles of Chilean wine, and talked about yacht deliveries, starting an adventure charter business in Belize and, no less, raising a family on a sailboat. We were touching on all the vital issues and certainly not wasting any time. By the time the sun nosed its way into the bedroom and we finally fell asleep, it was obvious that we had stumbled into one hell of a love affair.

The following evening, New Year's Eve, we went to South Beach, the revitalized Art Deco district in Miami Beach. Good fortune was indeed smiling on us: we found a nearby parking place. We made our way from sidewalk café to sidewalk café, laughing, loving, and dreaming.

As 1991 merged in 1992, I threw all caution to the wind and proposed. Lesa raised her eyebrows, a look of genuine surprise swept her face.

"Are you really asking me to marry you?"

That was a good question. Was I? I gazed off toward the ocean. The dark, lumpy horizon was sprinkled with splashes of white; the Gulf Stream was indiscriminately knocking off the tops of distant waves as a stiff northeast wind was rising. It seemed reassuring. The ocean has been my sounding board for many years. "This is crazy," I said to myself, "you hardly know her." But it seemed so right and besides, I was sure Neptune had a hand in this. There were too many unlikely twists of fate drawing us together. It was one of those moments in life that require decisiveness. I squared my shoulders, looked her right in the eyes and said,

"Yes, Lesa, I am asking you to marry me."

She smiled, kissed me gently and said, "I love you, John Kretschmer, and I will marry you." Then her eyes lit up and she continued. "But there are two conditions."

"What are they?"

"First, I want you to ask me again in the morning and secondly, I want you to buy me a hamburger right now because I'm starving."

Then she gave me another kiss. After a midnight snack, we found a room for the night and made love, the best kind of love when you are dreaming of sharing your lives together.

The first light of the new year came much too early and I awoke not only with a throbbing head but also to the shocking realization that although we hardly knew each other, we were now ostensibly engaged. Standing on the terrace, gulping powerful but good Cuban coffee, I felt a pang of deceit. Did Lesa realize that I was 33 years old and had never had a real job? Did she have a clue about how fiercely I guarded my independence from what I considered to be society's tentacles? Did she really understand what a vagabond I was? For more than 10 years, I had not spent 60 consecutive days in the United States. Did she know I'd written a book about another woman, a love story disguised as a sailing story? Believe me, that's a tough thing to have floating around and the only good thing about it was that it was finally going out of print. I knew that our engagement was about as official as a politician's campaign promise but I was sincere, I was in love. I was less concerned about our vague plans to marry one day than I was by the fact that there were so many things I hadn't told Lesa. I wanted this lovely woman to love me, not just my dreams. Unfortunately, the day-to-day, minute-by-minute reality of my life is not quite as alluring as the well-edited retelling of past adventures.

And, I had my secrets, mostly failures that I wasn't ready to share with anyone. Then, of course too, there was the delicate subject of my finances, or lack thereof. I made my living moving other people's sailboats from one side of an ocean to the other. And although I was damned good at it and supplemented my income by writing about my travels and adventures, this was not a job description that gives your future mother-in-law bragging rights at the country club. Mother-in-law? I didn't know anything about Lesa's family other than that they hailed from Oregon and judging from her family name and fair features, they had some Viking in their bloodlines. I optimistically assumed her forebears must have been bold pioneers to have made it all the way to the shores of the Pacific. My distant relatives ran out of steam in the Midwest.

I felt terribly guilty. There were so many confessions, unpaid bills and strange commitments, quiet fears and far-flung schemes. For the first and only time in my life, I felt like I needed a priest. Lesa joined me on the terrace and could tell something was troubling me. I started to ramble obliquely, trying and failing miserably to explain how I truly lived in and for the moment and wasn't

famous for long-range planning. Fortunately, Lesa interrupted me
and typically cut straight to the point.

"John, the most important thing is that we love each other,
now we have to come to know each other. I want to start by learning about this yacht-delivery business of yours."

"But do you still want to marry me?"

"It is the next morning, isn't it? Well, you kept your promise
and this may surprise you but, yes, I still want to marry you."

I wrapped her in my arms and said, "After you showed up in
San Pedro that morning with all your boxes, nothing you do surprises me."

There is no better way to get to know a person than on a sailboat, preferably one that is a long way from 7-Elevens, televisions
and telephones, and soon Lesa and I were winging our way toward
the Caribbean island nation of the Dominican Republic. One of my
steady accounts, a small sailboat brokerage run by a likable English-
man with a thick East End London accent, needed a big Irwin delivered from the Dominican Republic back to Fort Lauderdale. I
know Ted Irwin and have been through his plant on the west coast
of Florida, and I had no illusions about the quality of some of his
boats. But I also knew that most Irwins were better boats than their
reputations proclaimed and figured the 52-foot ketch would surely
survive an easy downwind run of about 1,000 miles. Besides, the
job paid well and although Lesa didn't know it and I had not let on,
I tended to live from delivery job to delivery job and from article to
article. Nothing makes a delivery skipper overlook the dubious quality of a boat faster than the prospect of a timely paycheck.

I should have been more suspect or at least more curious when
Joe, the broker, told me casually, "Something is a little funny down
there, John, something about unpaid bills. The owner, who is a
nice guy from Oklahoma, in the oil business I think, told me that
this talk of unpaid bills is a load of rubbish. Don't worry about it
but when you do get down there, be sure to let everyone know that
you are the owner's representative, put up a good show of presence, so to speak."

"A show of presence, Joe?"

"You know John, let 'em know you're the bloke in charge and
don't take any shit about unpaid bills."

Joe gave me 2,000 Dollars, or half the delivery fee, up front;

the exact location of the boat, named SIREN'S SONG; and the name of a local contact. We shook hands.

"I'll see you in a couple of weeks," I said casually and was on my way.

A typical delivery contract. I never doubted that if I did my job and delivered the boat back to Fort Lauderdale, I'd see the other half of the money and be reimbursed for unexpected expenses along the way. With luck I'd clear 3,000+ Dollars, which isn't bad for 10 days to two weeks' worth of work.

Boca Chica, a small beachfront collection of shabby hotels about 10 miles east of the capital, Santo Domingo, was utterly charmless. We hailed a rattletrap cab and made our way to a broken-down beach club, De Mar, where the boat was moored. At a tired tiki bar that looked like it might topple over in even a modest breeze, I inquired about Señor Gonzalez, our contact who was supposedly taking care of the boat. Nobody spoke English so I re-sorted to my jive Spanish, which is spoken entirely in the present tense, utilizing as few verb tenses as possible. But the surly bar-tender just shrugged his shoulders and the other patrons, com-pletely consumed by their rum drinks, ignored me. The boat was in plain view, less than 50 yards off the beach. Remembering Joe's advice to put up a show of presence, I decided to take possession of the boat with or without Señor Gonzalez's blessing.

I searched the beach for the boat's dinghy but it was not in sight. Undaunted, I dragged a rickety, abandoned old canoe to water's edge, told Lesa to throw our bags into it, and handed her a warped paddle. She looked dubious but I assured her that every-thing was fine and that this was standard yacht-delivery procedure. I was, after all, a professional. I launched the canoe into knee-deep water and after helping Lesa in, carefully stepped aboard and took up my paddle. Unfortunately, Lesa and I both leaned to the right to start paddling. Plop, over we went, capsized 10 feet from shore. The canoe broke in half and settled into the soft ooze as we waded ashore carrying our soaked belongings. I don't think this was the show of presence Joe had in mind.

After dragging what was left of the canoe ashore, I next com-mandeered a completely waterlogged pedal-boat that was half buried in the sand. With the help of Filito, a smiling young boy who was the only one around at all impressed with our show of presence, we managed to drag this unwieldy craft into the water. Filito and I peddled like maniacs while Lesa held onto our bags but the rudder was jammed and the useless boat had an annoying tendency to go in circles. Finally, after a dizzying 20-minute struggle, we reached SIREN'S SONG.

After tossing our bags aboard, Lesa noted sarcastically, "If our life together is going to be anything like our dinghy rides, we're in big trouble."

Our troubles on SIREN'S SONG were just beginning. The boat was locked and I did not have the key. Joe had assured me there was a full set of tools aboard so I had not bothered to lug my own. The dreary prospect of peddling back to shore inspired Lesa to become inventive and before long she was unscrewing the hinge behind the lock with a nail file. Within minutes, she had the companionway open and we slipped below. The interior of SIREN'S SONG was lovely and Lesa looked at me approvingly. As she marveled at the sunken galley, bright and spacious main saloon, and huge aft cabin with a centerline queen bunk, I noticed that the floorboards were ajar and suspected that something was amiss.

I had earlier observed from the beach that the boat's spars were stripped of sails and then, as I lifted the floorboards, my worst suspicions were confirmed. There were no batteries and the starter motor had been removed from the engine. We were not going to slip away quietly in SIREN'S SONG. Someone had made damned sure of that.

I was determined to keep my apprehensions about the boat to myself. This was Lesa's first delivery and I was foolishly hoping that this delivery would somehow defy the gods and go smoothly, and that Lesa would become enchanted with the sailing lifestyle. I should have known better. Like most gods, Neptune has a sardonic side. He could not resist testing her mettle.

As I have said before, optimism is vital in the yacht-delivery business. Indeed, with some of the boats I have delivered, blind optimism was required because if I had opened my eyes and looked too closely at the boats, I would never have left the dock. And while I suspected that we might be in for a small ordeal, I was confident that Señor Gonzalez would be able to explain why the boat had been stripped. Maybe it was a security measure? I was sure that he had the sails, batteries, and starter motor stashed away some-

place for safekeeping. The rest of the boat seemed in decent condition and once I ponied up a token bribe and made it clear that
the owner was not about to brook any more bullshit, I was sure
that we could put the boat back together in a day or two and then
quickly be underway. I have certainly paid my share of bribes over
the years. It was simply the modus operandi for this part of the
world and if you have a philosophical objection to paying bribes,
you might as well stay home because you will never get anything
accomplished. In some ways, I actually prefer the direct bribery tac-
tics of the Third World to the more cunning and devious methods
we've developed in the so-called 'First World'.

We decided to have dinner at the De Mar Club and wait for
Señor Gonzalez to turn up.

Halfway through the meal, a disheveled lady stormed into the
club screaming, "*Donde está el capitán norteamericano*? Where is
the Captain from America?"

More than a little surprised, I stood up and introduced myself.
The lady pulled on my arm and shouted in English, "Come, we
must save Señor Gonzalez. He is out there in the darkness on the
reef." Then she closed her eyes and crossed herself. "Please," she
insisted, "come quickly."

I gave Lesa an I-swear-I-have-never-seen-this-lady-before kind
of look as I followed her out the door. She gave me a half-laugh-
ing, half-concerned kind of look as I feebly waved good-bye.

We piled into her car and squealed off toward the yacht club
down the road. The lady finally introduced herself as Señora Gonzalez. Her husband had taken a recently repaired boat out for a test
sail and hit the treacherous reef that lies just beyond the harbor entrance. From the way she described the situation, his very survival
was in question.

"Why don't you call the police, or the coast guard, or somebody with a boat?" I asked, bewildered.

"Because I can't trust them."

Of course, I immediately wondered, if Señora Gonzalez doesn't
trust the police, why does she trust me? We parked the car and
sprinted down a narrow finger pier. We passed several nice-looking
sportfishing boats that would have been perfect for the rescue operation before finally coming to a little wooden skiff with an an-
cient-looking outboard motor perched on the stern.

"Please, get in." she screamed, "I'll cast off the lines."

As I jumped into the boat, I had a vague feeling that I was being set up for something.

"Start the engine," she demanded.

I pulled and pulled on the starter cord. Outboard motors are just not my thing. I don't know what it is about outboards but an otherwise perfectly running machine will simply refuse to run once it senses my presence in the boat. I tinkered with the choke and adjusted the throttle and pulled again. Nothing. Angry, I pulled even harder. Snap, I pulled the cord apart—I have the touch of a Russian midwife. Feeling like a failure in this time of dire need, I started to fit the oars into the locks and said gallantly, "Don't worry, I'll row."

Señora Gonzalez looked at me with hatred in her eyes, "But it is five miles to the reef."

"Oh, I see." I dropped the oars to the bottom of the boat.

I felt terrible and pictured Señor Gonzalez, a man I'd never met, a man without a first name apparently, flailing in the water, his boat foundering on the reef. I also wondered how his wife ever dreamed we'd survive a five-mile passage out to the reef in this rickety old skiff anyway.

Just then a young man, a boy really, in an open fishing boat came roaring alongside, spinning the wheel at the last minute, intentionally soaking us with his wake. While I seriously considered breaking his scrawny neck, Señora Gonzalez conversed with him in rapid Spanish. I only understood occasional descriptive words like *mierda* (shit). Then he gave us both a dirty sneer and zoomed away.

"Okay, I can take you back to the club. I hope I didn't disturb your dinner."

Señora Gonzalez's mood had completely changed; she was calm, eerily so.

I felt a cold dread and wondered if, God forbid, Señor Gonzalez was dead. In a whisper, I said, "He's not, well, you know?"

"No, he's fine."

"What? That's it then, the rescue is over?" I said in astonishment.

This lady is schizophrenic, I thought, and then I had a sudden fear that the entire event was orchestrated so that someone could abduct Lesa. No, I scolded myself, you're paranoid, or just in love.

"Yes, that boy will go fetch Señor Gonzalez. Please, let's go now."

She dropped me at the door of the club with a terse, "Thank you," and, without looking at me, extended a limp hand for me to shake and drove off. I staggered back to the table and tried to explain to Lesa what had happened.

"There is something strange going on here, isn't there, John?"

"Yes," I confessed, "but don't worry, we will sort out everything in the morning."

"But what about Señor Gonzalez?"

"To hell with him. Come on, let's paddle out to the boat."

"I have a better idea, let's swim out to the boat. It will be faster."

The following afternoon we finally pinned down Señor Gonzalez who was obviously avoiding us and the plot began to thicken. From the jaunty Greek fisherman's cap on his head to the nautical belt with signal flags encircling an expanded midsection, Señor Gonzalez had the look of a sailor who was clearly more comfortable ashore than at sea. Yet he seemed harmless; indeed, he was quite likable. His harrowing encounter with the reef wasn't nearly as dire as his wife had made it out to be. Later, we learned the truth about that night. It seems Señor Gonzalez and his new partners were celebrating the arrival of the American captain, namely me. My arrival promised to bring in either a windfall in phony repair bills, or better yet, a fortune in extortion. They celebrated a little too heartily, however, and in a drunken stupor, they hit the reef on the way back into the harbor. They had to be towed off in what would prove to be a costly bit of seamanship.

Señor Gonzalez was ready to put the previous night's mishap out of his mind and initially he refused to discuss the matter. However, his financial troubles were not as easy to forget. After a few drinks at the lopsided tiki bar, he started to spill his story. It seems he had recently sold his interest in the De Mar Club to three 'investors' from Santo Domingo and he was obviously being pressured about something. I had a distinct feeling that Lesa and I had arrived in Boca Chica at just the wrong time. Something devious was in the works and I had a hunch that we were going to be involved in the drama. For someone whose job is simply to deliver sailboats from point A to point B, I have a knack of getting mixed up in other people's business.

Señor Gonzalez apologized for his wife's bizarre behavior the night before. "She is not herself these days," he explained. "None of us are."

The good señor matched his wife's flair for the dramatic. "She doesn't know what I am going through," he complained. "She has no idea and now I have to repair their boat after hitting that stupid reef."

He wiped his brow. Señor Gonzalez was a talker and I am a listener and little by little he explained his dilemma. The bottom line was that he had promised more than he could deliver when he sold the club and his boat-repair business. I had heard stories about the ruthless nature of the Dominican Republic mob and Señor Gonzalez had the nervous look and sweaty palms of someone who had made a pact with the devil. When he presented me with several pages of work orders, explaining "there is this small matter of a few unpaid bills," I suddenly realized that SIREN'S SONG and her distant gringo owner's checkbook represented his chance to step back from the abyss.

Glancing at the sheets of paper, I quickly scanned down the list until I came to the final number, 14,000 Dollars. From my brief survey of the boat, I knew immediately that this was a complete scam. Looking more closely at the work order, I realized that maybe 2,000 Dollars was legitimate. I also noticed that the owner had not signed the work order, someone else had.

"Who is this?" I asked, pointing to the signature.

"That is the former captain," Señor Gonzalez explained. "He commissioned the work."

I decided to call his bluff right away.

"This is a joke and you know it. What will you settle for and when can I get the batteries, starter motor, and the sails?"

"Don't insult me, Captain, I personally supervised this work. I will not accept anything but full payment. And cash payment, in U.S. Dollars."

Señor Gonzalez was not hostile, he was desperate, and there wasn't room in his voice for apparent compromise. I told him I had to call the owner and would get back to him. I realized that poor Señor Gonzalez was on the verge of a complete breakdown. I remained stern but calm. I knew that this money was not destined for his pocket. I had a strong hunch that he was an honorable man. If I played things right, when all was said and done, he would end up on my side in this strange affair.

I phoned Joe back in Fort Lauderdale and explained the situation. He was outraged and asked me to fax a copy of the bill and to sit tight while he contacted the owner. Later that day, Lesa and I had the opportunity to meet the new owners of the De Mar Club. Three oily-skinned thugs, dressed in tight pants, silk shirts and gold chains, invited us to join them at the bar. The young boy whom I had seen the night before during the ill-fated rescue attempt was also there. The leader, an unpleasant-looking fellow who could have doubled as Manuel Noriega, poured me a drink, Bacardi on the rocks, light on the rocks.

"Captain," he said with a gravely voice and a thin smile, "I understand we have a small disagreement."

Before I could say anything, he waved his hand and continued.

"Please, let us drink to friendship, at least for today anyway. Tomorrow, I am afraid, is something we cannot know."

As Lesa and I warily toasted our swarthy companions, I had to suppress a giggle. I felt like a character in an old Edward G. Robinson film. However, I was soon to learn that this pockmarked philosopher was in the process of hatching a nasty plan. After pouring another round of drinks, he showed me a crumbled piece of paper that he had obviously lifted from the boat. It seems that SIREN'S SONG had been left too long in the Dominican Republic. Not only had her cruising permit expired, but according to the fine print, if she didn't leave the country soon, she might not leave at all.

"You see," General Noriega explained, "if your friend does not pay his bill, we will have no option other than to confiscate the boat. It is a matter of national security. We can't have you Americans leaving your yachts in our beautiful country. We have been forced to file a lien of repossession with our coast guard. But, please, don't take this personally. Why don't you and your lady friend join us for dinner?"

We declined the invitation and retreated to the boat.

"John, this is crazy and it sounds serious too. Is this really your problem?"

Lesa's question was valid. Why was I becoming embroiled in

this mess and in the process, involving her? I also wondered, does the Dominican Republic even have a coast guard?

"Well baby, if we don't do something about this, the owner may well lose his boat. I have a feeling that he should just give these guys their 14,000 Dollar bribe and get his boat out of here as soon as possible. I'm sure they're hoping he won't do that and then they can 'legally' confiscate the boat, which is worth close to 200,000 Dollars even in a fire sale."

"But that's extortion."

I just nodded.

"Is this what all yacht deliveries are like?"

"No, baby, not at all. Usually the boats are in perfect condition and I just pitch my gear aboard, cast off the lines, mix a cold drink and sail off into the sunset."

"Ya, right."

The next morning I called Joe and he informed me that the owner was furious, not only with the Dominican bandits but also with his former captain, who, it seems, had pissed away a rather large insurance claim. He refused to pay the bill. I listened patiently and then frankly explained the rapidly incubating plan to confiscate the boat.

Joe moaned, exasperated, "Sorry about this one, John," he said. "Just sit tight until you hear from me. And by the way, I owe you one after this. I'll find you a nice boat to take to Europe this spring."

Joe called back straightaway. "Okay, he'll send the money, John, a certified bank check. If that's not good enough, tell them to go to hell and we'll contact the U.S. Consulate." Then Joe added in an unusually serious tone, "But make damned sure you get the sails, starter motor, batteries and anything else you need before you give them the money."

The check arrived by air courier the next day. After leaving instructions to have the boat ready to sail in two days, Lesa and I rented a Jeep and disappeared into the mountainous hinterland of lovely Hispaniola. Although I was a bit nervous carrying around in my pocket a 14,000 Dollar check that was as good as cash, soon we were high above the sea, switchbacking our way toward the little village of Constanza, which, according to our map, was literally at the end of the road. The only thing west of Constanza was the Haiti frontier. It seemed like a safe spot to spend a few days.

The once-saintly, now much-beleaguered Admiral of the Ocean Sea, old Chris Columbus, stumbled upon Hispaniola exactly 500 years before us. He was enchanted and described the island as "the fairest land human eyes have ever seen." Columbus, who had a royal patron to impress and an advertising copywriter's command of sappy adjectives, was prone to exaggeration, but with Hispaniola his description was not far off. The lush coastline gave way to stands of pines and the temperature became refreshingly cool as the little Jeep labored up to a mountain pass at nearly 8,000 feet.

The second largest island in the Caribbean (Cuba is the largest), Hispaniola has had a turbulent history. Today the island is shared by the Dominican Republic, which occupies the eastern two-thirds, and Haiti, which covers what's left to the west. The division is symbolic of a divided past. Haiti, which was one of the first independent nations in the Western Hemisphere, has had almost continual turmoil and repression since its founding in 1804 and the Dominican Republic has worked hard to keep pace. Spain, France, a succession of pirates, Haiti and the United States have all invaded and occupied the Dominican Republic. Haiti had the despised, despotic Duvalier family to guide her through most of this century, while the Dominican Republic had an equally brutal tyrant at the helm, Rafael Trujillo. Both Trujillo and his successor, Joaquin Balaguer, were masters at paying lip service to democracy and squeezing aid out of the United States. Fortunately, both of these regimes have crumbled and fledgling democracies have taken tenuous roots on both sides of Hispaniola today.

The Jeep finally descended into a large, fertile valley and we made our way into Constanza. We had been dreaming of staying at the spa that was advertised on splashy billboards every five miles from Santo Domingo. Soaking in hot mineral springs seemed the perfect tonic after a couple of stressful days. But when we got to the spa, it turned out to be a wreck of unfinished cement buildings beside a dried-up creek bed. It seems they had invested all of their startup capital in billboards. Instead, we found a charming cabana, and after a stroll around town where baseball caps and cowboy boots were the latest fashion and dominoes the game of choice, we retired to our snug cabin for the night. As darkness fell, we buried ourselves beneath a pile of woolen covers; it was surprisingly cold. Soon, however, we generated some heat of our own and held each other close. Although one can never be certain of these things, we feel pretty sure that a seed was planted that night in the mountains of Hispaniola.

Anxious to make sure the work was progressing on the boat, we returned to Boca Chica the following night. Nothing had been done. I am a patient man but my patience was exhausted. I stormed into Señor Gonzalez's office and demanded to know what was going on. He started to hem and haw before I cut him short.

"Here is the check," I said, pulling it out of my pocket and waving it in front of his face. "I want the starter motor and batteries installed and the sails on the boat by this time tomorrow. If they're not, then Lesa and I catch the next flight home and you can deal with your nice new friends and with your conscience."

Finally, the following morning we started to make progress. The boat was towed to the yacht club and a mechanic dispatched to install the starter and batteries. Normally, I would have done this work myself, but I felt I should at least get some service for 14,000 Dollars. Lesa and I did rig the sails and prepare the boat for sailing. Unfortunately, the starter motor failed to crank the diesel and had to be rebuilt, which meant yet another day's delay.

After stashing the check in the headliner in the forward cabin, Lesa and I hiked to a beachfront hotel where they had arranged an outdoor barbecue. The food smelled delicious and we had dinner. Later that night, we were both raked with cramps. Something we'd eaten was bad and we were both experiencing severe food poisoning symptoms. It was awful; fortunately the boat had more than one head so we endured our miseries in private. In between bouts of nausea and diarrhea, we complained that this was surely General Noriega's doing.

Lesa and I awoke feeling wretched but by the end of the day SIREN'S SONG was at last ready to depart. To his credit, Señor Gonzalez worked hard and personally drove the mechanic all over Santo Domingo searching for parts to rebuild the starter. However, by the time we paid him and obtained a reluctant clearance from customs, it was dark, as night falls early in the tropics. We didn't care. We were determined to leave and Señor Gonzalez arranged for a guide to lead us out past the reef through an intricate, unmarked channel. I figured if we put the boat on a reef at this point, it was meant to be. Our pilot turned out to be the same young boy whom I had wanted to strangle earlier. Following his dim flashlight on an otherwise unlit dinghy, we wound our way out to sea.

Fortunately, the night was calm and we set an offshore course to gain sea room. I was feeling dreadful and although Lesa was feeling only slightly better, I gave her a heading to steer, instructions to watch out for ships and, after hastily appointing her captain for the night, collapsed below. I was thoroughly exhausted. Although Lesa had never stood a night watch alone before, I knew she could handle it. And she did, although it really wasn't necessary to alter course for the crescent moon that suddenly nosed above the black horizon.

The next day, as we glided through the Mona Passage, Lesa cornered me in the cockpit.

"Okay, Capitán Norteamericano, that wasn't very nice to leave me in the cockpit last night, I was scared. It is time for a little payback. I think there are some things you haven't told me about the yacht delivery business."

"What do you mean?" I said, laughing. We were both feeling a little better.

"You know what I mean. As far as I can tell we have at least six days of sailing in front of us. I want to hear the whole story, the good, the bad and the ugly. You've spent the last 15 years sailing all over the world. I want to hear about it and I want the truth."

"The truth can be pretty elusive, you know," I said defensively.

Lesa shook her head. She was serious.

"You want to hear it all?"

She nodded.

"You want to hear about how I almost sank in the Gulf Stream, was shot at by communist lunatics in the Arabian Sea, went through the eye of Hurricane Bob, survived Typhoon Roy, nearly sank again, this time in the North Atlantic, and all that kind of stuff?"

"Now we are getting somewhere," Lesa said approvingly and gave me a kiss.

"Do you want to hear about the other girl? I mean, she was a great sailor and a big part of some of these trips, you know."

Lesa looked away. Then she turned back smiling, "Well you can leave out what you see fit on that one, but you have to stick to the facts. Don't just tell me what you think. I'll want to hear, no candy coating."

I cracked open two lukewarm Presidentes, the local beer of the Dominican Republic, adjusted the autopilot, and scanned the horizon. We owned the ocean, or at least the five or six miles of it that I could see.

"Okay, baby, here goes. I guess it all began because I was famous."

CHAPTER 3

Famous

There are certain queer times and occasions in this strange mixed affair we call life when a man takes this whole universe for a vast practical joke, though the wit thereof he dimly discerns, and more than suspects that the joke is at nobody's expense but his own.

HERMAN MELVILLE, Moby Dick

MAYOR FEINSTEIN SENT her young assistant to present the keys to the city. It was a typical spring day in San Francisco, cold, windy and gray. The quickly organized ceremony on a wobbly dock at the Pier 39 marina looked a lot better on television later that night than it did in the drizzly reality of the morning. Thanks to video editing, however, my soon-to-be-adoring public was none the wiser. I was well on my way to becoming famous. While I already knew that fame is about as enduring as the unrefrigerated shelf life of sushi, I think that Andy Warhol was a cynic. My worldwide celebrity lasted for the better part of two weeks.

It was early May 1984 and I had just sailed from New York by way of Cape Horn in a Contessa 32 sloop. The winsome Contessa is a damned fine boat, but an absurdly small one for so ambitious an undertaking. The 16,000-mile windward slog (the subject of my book *Cape Horn to Starboard*) retraced the outbound route of the legendary gold-rush clipper ships of the 1850s. Although we didn't establish any records worth mentioning without asterisks, we did survive Neptune's fury and a young skipper's many mistakes—plus my corporate sponsor, Stroh's Brewery, was delighted that we had sense enough to arrive on a slow news day.

I didn't expect an armada of pleasure boats to greet us, or a watery throng to welcome us home as did the one that embraced my hero Sir Francis Chichester in Plymouth, England. But I was hoping that maybe a few spirited sailors, having heard of our voyage, would brave the elements to catch a glimpse of us gliding

GIGI, a Contessa 32, arriving in San Francisco after a 16,000-mile voyage from New York via Cape Horn.

beneath the Golden Gate Bridge. But when that dramatic arch spanning the mouth of San Francisco Bay finally loomed and the end of our protracted voyage was within reach, there was not a single sail, not a single vessel in sight. In fact, it would have been a great time to be smuggling something sinister into San Francisco because we had the bay to ourselves. After we were well past the bridge, a rusty fishing trawler lumbered alongside and gave us a salute as we hoisted our faded red spinnaker. But they couldn't see us for long as a thick fog clamped down on the bay. Soon after, however, a helicopter from the local CBS station emerged out of the gloom. It whirled overhead, spoiling our wind as we drifted in and out of the fog.

A launch with a few greenish newspaper reporters and the public relations agent hired by Stroh's popped out of the fog to lead us to a slip at the swanky Pier 39 marina. My crew Bill Oswald and I had been at sea for 72 days and we were not very steady on our feet as we climbed onto the floating dock. We had completely exhausted our stores, existing for more than a week on vegetables from the few rusty cans we had left on board. These were the worst, the ones I always ate last: lima beans, wax beans, and asparagus. While I was dreaming of many things, from the obvious to a cold beer and a greasy cheeseburger, I must admit that the keys to the city were not high on my list. But fame waits for no man, not even a bearded, bedraggled 25-year-old kid from the suburbs masquerading as an old salt.

Unfortunately, the ceremony did not go well. The mayor's assistant was nervous and worried more about the rain ruining his hairdo than the job at hand. I was shaky, to say the least. After a brief speech proclaiming 'GIGI Arrival Day' to the six people milling about the dock, the mayor's assistant presented me with a plaque and then hastily handed over the keys. I dropped them. They started to blow down the dock. I ran after them and nimbly stepped on them before they blew into the water. You see, what I didn't at first realize was that they were Styrofoam. Squeal, crunch. Oops. We managed to piece them back together and after reenacting the ceremony for the TV crew, quickly retreated to a nearby pub to reacquaint ourselves with our sponsor's product.

In some ways, the voyage had become a personal disappoint-

GIGI clearing the Golden Gate Bridge.

ment. I had hoped to equal the average sailing time of a clipper ship, 120 days. But when we staggered into San Francisco Bay, we were 162 days out from New York Harbor and the snail like progress of the last leg of the voyage had eroded the huge satisfaction of rounding the Horn. But today, with the perspective of 15 years and more than 200,000 bluewater miles later, I view the voyage more fondly and, I believe, more accurately.

Considering that my total offshore experience before the Cape Horn Clipper Ship Expedition, as we grandiloquently dubbed it, was a measly tradewind transatlantic crossing and some Caribbean sailing, the fact that we managed to bash our way around the Horn against the wind and currents at all is rather impressive. When you consider that our little 32-foot Contessa, GIGI, weighed about 10,000 pounds fully laden and had only 28 inches of freeboard, the voyage becomes more commendable, and more idiotic. Our 11-day doubling of the Horn, or sailing nonstop from the 50th parallel in the Atlantic to the same parallel in the Pacific, remains one of the fastest on record for any sailing vessel. And I navigated with my sextant: This was the age before the GPS and even SatNav for that matter. Besides, it doesn't matter how much I boast about the voyage today because at the time Dan Rather thought it was a great accomplishment, and what could be a more accurate barometer of importance than that?

The hotel operator was nonplussed, "CBS News is on the line, can you hold for Dan Rather?" I was lying on the bed in the Sheraton Hotel trying to figure out if it was moving or if I was. After holding for what seemed like an hour, Dan Rather's distinctive, earnest and familiar voice chimed in, "Welcome home, Don."

"Thanks, Dan," I said modestly and quietly corrected him. "It's John, with a J."

"Right, John. That was some trip."

"It sure was, Dan." I was pretty sure that Dan not only had no idea who I was but also had no idea why he was calling me. I could hear a voice in the background, his producer probably, giving him some of the details of our voyage.

"Well, we'd like to have you and your crew on our new morning show in New York tomorrow."

"That would be terrific, Dan, but we're in San Francisco."

After a short pause I could hear Dan say, "They're in San Francisco." The other voice, somewhat irritated, replied, "I know they're in San Francisco, Dan. Tell him we'll have a limo at the hotel tonight and fly them to the city, first class. We'll put them up at the Essex House and fly them back after the show."

Dan dutifully relayed the instructions and I hastily agreed.

"Well, once again, welcome home, Don, and we'll see you in New York."

"Thanks a lot, Dan."

The newly launched CBS morning show was struggling, unable to compete with ABC's popular *Good Morning America* and NBC's long-standing *Today Show*. In an attempt to boost ratings and, I guess, convince potential guests to forsake the others and sign on their show, CBS brass enlisted Dan Rather to issue the invitations. It sure worked with me. I quickly called the public relations agent Stroh's had arranged in San Francisco and relayed the good news. He was ecstatic. There was, however, a small matter he had to discuss with me. It seemed the *National Enquirer* had become very interested in our story and was willing to offer me 5,000 Dollars for exclusive rights, which meant we would not be able to talk with any other media. The public relations agent urged me to forgo the *Enquirer*'s offer, suggesting that they would turn some aspect of the trip into highly sensationalized nonsense. I turned down the offer but had fun dreaming up potential headlines.

"Only a can of wax beans keeps sailors from turning cannibalistic!"

"Aliens visit sailboat while becalmed in the doldrums!"

"Mermaid sues sailors for sexual harassment!"

Bill Oswald wanted no part of CBS's offer. Having spent 72 days together and having lost close to 1,000 games of Yahtzee, Oz was ready to put some distance between the two of us. He jumped into his Corvette and sped off toward his Texas home. Ty Techera, GIGI's owner and my crew member for the Cape Horn leg, was in Africa on business. Only Molly Potter, my girlfriend/wife, and I piled into the limo, and sampled the wet bar on the way to the airport. That slash after girlfriend requires an explanation, of course. Molly and I had been living together for three years before the Cape Horn trip and she sailed with me on the first leg from New York to Rio de Janeiro. En route, in fact not far from Cape Horn, I proposed via single sideband radio and she flew down to meet me in Chile. We tried to get married but Chilean law required that we be residents in the country for 90 days before we could officially obtain a marriage license. With divorce illegal in Chile in those days, the authorities took a dim view of two non-Catholic gringos trying to organize a makeshift marriage ceremony. In the end, we had our own private ceremony, invoking the youthful mantra: "What good is a piece of paper when it comes to love and marriage anyway?" As things turned out, however, Chilean officials may have known what they were talking about because our so-called marriage never took root.

After a night in the Essex House penthouse suite, we made our way to CBS studios on West 57th Street. We would be interviewed by Meredith Vierra, sandwiched between baseball manager Sparky Anderson and ratings guru A.C. Nielsen. We were sitting nervously in the studio waiting room, expecting some instruction or coaching when suddenly we were led to a couple of easy chairs and had microphones pinned to our sweaters. Then the lights came on as if we were in Yankee Stadium, and we were on the air.

The interview was stilted, to say the least. I was totally unprepared for Meredith's questions and, although she was obviously a professional, she knew little about sailing. I tended to give clipped, factual, one-word answers to her questions. I hadn't learned that accuracy was far less important than smart one-liners.

Finally, her pleasant smile masking desperation with an obviously dull interview, she asked, "So why did you do it, why sail around Cape Horn?"

By this time, I was beginning to relax. I leaned back in my chair and said, "Meredith, that is a good question, a seemingly simple question but a hard one to answer."

Just as I was about to launch into a philosophical explanation, which no doubt would have eventually hearkened all the way back to Francis Chichester, I saw her roll her eyes and start to go over notes for her next interview with A. C. Nielsen. So I gave the short answer. "Well, it was something I really wanted to do." And then bingo, off to a commercial break and within minutes we were out on the street.

We wandered around Manhattan for a few hours in a daze. To my complete astonishment, somebody recognized me as we milled around the Barnes and Noble bookstore on Third Avenue and clapped me on the shoulder, "Great interview this morning!" I was shocked. Hell, I was famous. Invigorated by my new celebrity, I mustered the courage to call a literary agent who had been recommended by a friend. I mentioned that I'd just come from the CBS studios—the magic words—and set up an afternoon appointment. I was more nervous about meeting the agent in his elegant Upper East Side brownstone than I had been about appearing on TV. In my life, even as a kid, television never had much meaning. I rarely tuned in. But books were, and still are, another matter. There was something sacred about printed words bound between two covers, and meeting somebody to talk about a book deal made my heart race.

The agent lit his pipe and cut straight to the point.

"So how much media can you generate? How strong are your television contacts? Books today are all about promotion. You need to get back on television a year from now when your book comes out, otherwise it will be out of print in three months. Television is everything."

Trying to conceal my disappointment—I thought we'd be discussing narrative styles and story outlines—I said, "Well, I know
Dan Rather and A.C. Nielsen."

"You know Dan Rather!"

"Yes, he called me when we arrived in San Francisco."

The fact that Dan and I were tight (I decided not to mention that Dan thought my name was Don) was music to the
agent's ears and he urged me to get him an outline and sample
chapters as soon as possible. "You're looking at a five-figure advance," he assured me. What I didn't realize at the time was that
a five-figure advance was entirely relative to where the decimal
point was placed.

That evening we dined with my friend Edd Kalehoff, a successful composer and producer. Edd treated us to a celebration
dinner at Tavern on the Green. Earlier in the day, the public relations agent in San Francisco told me that he was trying to
arrange radio interviews while I was in New York and to keep him
posted as to our whereabouts. I tried to remain nonchalant when
the waiter came over to the table and said that WNBC was calling and wanted to do a live interview. He brought the phone to
the table and as the savvy-yet-hungry celebrity that I was, I conducted the interview while munching on the croutons in my
salad.

Back in San Francisco, we returned to a full schedule of television and radio appearances. The public relations agent, who despite his life's calling was a nice guy, was certainly doing his job.
I was a guest on a show called TGIF, a popular afternoon talk
show in the Bay Area. The hostess was a giggling bleached blond
who was geographically challenged. "Today," she announced in
her squeaky voice, "we'll meet a man who sailed around Cape
Horn," adding with an informed air, "You know, those boisterous waters off the southern tip of Africa." At one point in the interview, she asked me how I felt after I was pitched overboard
during a capsize. I replied, "wet," which was about the funniest
thing she had ever heard and she giggled right into a commercial
break. For some reason, I appeared at a Greek festival and also
conducted a few more radio interviews, answering the same questions over and over again but additional television shows were

canceled. It had been less than a week and my act was already wearing thin on the West Coast.

It was time to head to Detroit, where Stroh's had their corporate offices and my hometown. "Your story will still be hot there," the public relations agent assured me, as though my self-esteem ebbed and flowed with the status of my media popularity.

We made the rounds of the talk shows in Detroit and after I gave one stirring version of the voyage, I was even invited to be a regular on *Kelly and Company*. By this time I knew what punch lines worked and I found that I was better with a live audience. I lifted host John Kelly in his chair, angled him over about 30 degrees, and shook him up and down to give him a graphic idea of what it was like aboard GIGI. The audience, comprised almost entirely of middle-aged women, shrieked, and shrieking audiences mean good programming on sappy talk shows. I appeared with exercise guru Richard Simmons and Dr. Joyce Brothers. While Richard worried about the long-term effects of washing hair in salt water, Dr. Brothers suspected that I had some type of sexual hangup and that was why I had to prove myself by rounding Cape Horn.

"Adventurers usually feel secretly inadequate," she told the audience while I sat in the easy chair next to her smiling like an imbecile. Later, when I saw the tape, I laughed because there was no mistaking who I was or what my hangups were. As Dr. Brothers spoke, the camera focused on me with the words, 'John Kretschmer—Adventurer', plastered across the close-up shot. Fortunately, they didn't place my hangups, in numerical order, under my name.

The public relations agent was right: I was still hot in Detroit. On Monday, I was front-page news in both papers, *The Detroit News* and *The Free Press*, and had a long interview with legendary radio host J.P. McCarthy, who, amazingly, compared me to Odysseus. On Tuesday, I met Bob Seger while, for some reason, being interviewed on a rock-and-roll station. On Wednesday, I signed a deal with a speaker's bureau and, on Thursday, talked with video producers about appearing in a learn-to-sail production. By Friday, I was almost forgotten. The following Monday, I reached the bottom.

I agreed to appear on a small radio program, broadcast out of Sarnia, Ontario, just across the St. Clair River from Port Huron at the base of Michigan's thumb. The producer had told me that the host was a knowledgeable sailor and that the show, which featured live call-ins, was very popular. "A lot of these people used to work in the auto plants, now they're out of work so they have nothing better to do than to call our show," he said. That was reassuring. I turned up at the appointed time and was led into the studio. The host was already on the air when I quietly sat down. He was so excited he couldn't help letting on to his listeners that I was his next guest.

"We have an exciting guest coming up after the commercial break," he warned the audience. "You bet we do. He is right here in the studio ready to answer your questions about his amazing, record-breaking sailing voyage."

It was a relief to finally have an interviewer who apparently seemed to know something about sailing and what our expedition was all about. He clapped me on the shoulder, "Great to have you here," and ran to the toilet during the short break. By the time he was back in his seat, he was on the air again and continuing his introduction.

"Sitting next to me, ladies and gentlemen, is an amazing man, a man who in many ways is a worthy successor to Christopher Columbus, Ferdinand Magellan, and the other great explorers who bravely plied the world's oceans long before they were charted."

At first I thought to myself, he's getting a bit carried away but that's just the way these media people are. But a successor to Columbus, for God's sake? Soon however, I suspected that something was wrong.

"This man, right here, yes sir, sitting next to me, with two younger companions, this man completed an absolutely amazing voyage in a 37-foot steel boat."

Now I was worried because his facts were all wrong. But he blundered on.

"Today, we are privileged to have John Kretschmer in our studios, the man who sailed nonstop around the world without any instrumentation at all. That's right, no electronics, no compass, nothing, only the same instincts that guided primitive man, the instincts that guide seabirds. John, it's nice to have you with us."

The stunned look on my face didn't detour the loose-tongued host and before long, the first calls were coming in. It finally dawned on me what was happening. About the same time that we completed our trip around Cape Horn, another far more impressive expedition was also just winding up. A chap named Marvin Creamer, a professor from New Jersey, completed a non-stop, instrument-free circumnavigation. Creamer was an expert in natural navigation, but his amazing voyage never received the attention it warranted. His boat however, a Goderich 37, was built right up the road from Sarnia, which explained why the radio host knew so much about his voyage. Marvin Creamer was a hero in southern Ontario. Unfortunately, I wasn't Marvin Creamer. Or was I?

I was. It just didn't seem right to make the host seem like a complete idiot; he was so excited. Hell, I knew a lot about natural navigation. So for the next 30 minutes, I answered questions about sailing around the world without using any instruments. By the time I staggered out of the studio and into my car, I realized that it was time to be something other than famous.

Driving home, I took stock of my situation. Although I was officially 'an adventurer' (complete with the requisite sexual hangups), the sobering reality was that I was 25 years old, a multiple-time college drop-out, virtually broke, and the only thing I knew how to do was sail. The Midwest was closing in on me. I had to get back to the ocean. I stopped at my mom's house long enough to round up Molly, gather our few possessions and continued south at full throttle. Twenty-four hours later, I was back in Fort Lauderdale.

I visited a few yacht brokers, looking for captain's work but nothing materialized. Following the time-worn lead of down-and-out sailors, I retreated to the liquor store to invest a few of my dwindling dollars in a bottle of liquid therapy, specifically, the cheapest gin I could find. I think it was Popov's. As I ambled up to the counter, the store manager, a former neighbor who lived on a small sailboat, shouted, "John, wow man, I saw you on television. Hey that was great." Rich, it turns out had closely followed our Cape Horn exploits. "You're famous, man."

"I know."

"What are you buying this rot gut for?" he asked as he rang up the purchase.

"Oh, it's a for a friend. He told me to pick up a bottle of cheap gin and this is cheap."

He accepted my obvious fib with a nod and then launched into another subject.

"GIGI was built in England, wasn't she?"

"Ya, in Lymington. Why?"

"Well, you see, the dollar is very strong right now, especially against the pound and I was thinking about buying a bigger boat in England."

"Really." Rich, who runs a great liquor store, comes from a long line of retailers. However, he also has a bit of a paunch, a Ph.D. in anthropology, and is a specialist on Ming Dynasty pottery. He did not strike me as someone who would enjoy a transatlantic passage, but you never can tell.

"You know a lot about English boats, don't you John?"

"Probably more than most Americans, and I know the south coast of the U.K. quite well. Why?"

"Let me take you to lunch."

We retreated next door to the Southport Raw Bar. Before the conch chowder arrived, Rich was earnestly sketching the lines of his ultimate boat on a cocktail napkin.

"That looks like a Fisher," I said jokingly. "You know one of those North Sea pilothouse things."

I was about to add, "You don't want one of those tubs," when Rich cut in excitedly, "Exactly, you do know your boats, that's what I want. That's my dream boat. I never thought I could afford one but now with the exchange rate, I think I can manage, depending on you, of course, a decent used 34-foot or maybe even a 37-foot."

"What do you mean, depending on me?"

"You see, I don't have the time to spend looking for the boat, fitting it out and then sailing it back to Florida. I've been looking for the right person, someone I can trust and who has the sailing experience. When you came into the store, I knew you were the man for job."

"Wait a minute. You want me to go to England, find you a

boat, buy it for you, get it ready and then sail it back to Lauderdale?"

"Exactly. Would you consider it and what would you charge?"

"Rich, this will take two to three months."

"I know, that's okay."

"And we'll have to get going soon to be back before hurricane season revs up."

"I'm ready for you to leave tomorrow."

"Wow, um, how does 5,000 Dollars plus expenses sound?"

I was so anxious for the job I would have done it for expenses only, but when Rich's eyes lit up and he agreed immediately, I knew that I had charged much too little. But I didn't care. I was in the yacht-delivery business and, more importantly, I was headed back to sea.

*   *   *

The autopilot sang SIREN'S SONG like a tone-deaf drunk, weaving all over the ocean. The dark outline of Hispaniola was just visible off the port beam as Lesa returned to the cockpit with two cold Presidentes. I took the helm, the beer, and a moment to admire the beautiful woman I had fallen so madly in love with. Lesa read my thoughts.

"You know, Captain, I get the feeling that you're kind of lucky, that things just fall into your lap."

I smiled. I was thinking the same thing. How else would I have stumbled upon her in Belize? When you factored the odds of us meeting, you had to believe in either luck or predetermination. But she was thinking of other things.

"Being lucky is not always good. I mean, I know you are a great sailor but there are probably a lot of sailors who would love to deliver boats but have never had the chance. They don't know the right people. They never had somebody hand them 5,000 Dollars and a plane ticket to England. I know you proved yourself by rounding Cape Horn, of course, but that feat alone didn't give you an exclusive right to sail for a living. You need some luck to do that too."

I scanned the horizon, took a slug of beer and thought about her statement for a while. At first I thought she was still mad at me for abandoning her in the cockpit the night before, then I realized it reflected upon a major difference in our personalities. After a bitter divorce ripped her family apart, Lesa moved out of the house at age 18 and has supported herself ever since. Nothing has come easy; she didn't have a safety net, as I did, to cushion the fall of youthful fantasies run amok. She moved from Oregon to California and made her way in the world. Yet, she was willing to walk away from a hard-hewed, top sales job and move, lock, stock, and five boxes' worth, to Belize.

"I guess I am lucky, Lesa, in a way I've always been lucky. But there is one thing that I've learned about luck. It rears its head as an opportunity, not a gift, and what seems to separate the lucky from the unlucky is the willingness to take Lady Luck for a ride."

Lesa smiled. One of the best aspects of love, especially early on, is that you tend to agree with each other. "Okay, I'll buy that, for now anyway. Tell me about the ride Lady Luck, disguised as a liquor store manager, threw your way."

CHAPTER 4

Yacht Delivery 101

If a man must be obsessed by something, I suppose a boat is as good as anything, perhaps a bit better than most.

E.B. WHITE, The Sea and Wind That Blows

"WHY DON'T WE RETIRE to the inner sanctum," English yacht broker Dennis Lowes suggested. We ignored the icy glare and obvious disgust of Dennis' lovely but proper secretary, who, according to rumor, occasionally doubled as his wife. We slipped into the book-lined back room of what was once-legendary yacht designer Laurent Giles' office in a quaint High Street row house in Lymington. Dennis offered me a thick cigar, a glass of brandy that took my breath away, and some advice.

"John, you'd better give up looking for a Fisher, you bloody Americans have snapped them all up."

"But Dennis, my client is really looking to buy a Fisher 34, or at least a Fisher 30. If I can't find one, he'll be so disappointed, and more importantly, I'll be out of a job."

"Oh, don't be so specific, a motorsailer is a motorsailer. They don't sail or motor well, especially the short fat ones. We have plenty of other boats that fit that description. Just pick something with a pilothouse or a deck saloon and be done with it."

Molly and I had arrived at Gatwick Airport a week earlier and had spent our time combing the coast, from Ipswich to Plymouth, looking for a Fisher 34. Rich who, as far as I knew, used his limited vacation time to ply the Florida coast and occasionally the Bahamas, for some quixotic reason, had his heart set on owning one of the stubby, massively constructed motorsailers built along the lines of a North Sea trawler. I guess somewhere, deep in his soul,

Rich (like a lot of us) saw himself as a Viking just biding time managing a liquor store.

I had met Dennis Lowes on a previous trip to England and promised him that if I ever returned to the U.K. to buy a boat, he would be my broker. He probably came to regret that I kept my word as we planted ourselves on the plush couches in his office after each excursion and kept him busy searching for any and all Fishers for sale. His wife, who no doubt had the sharper business acumen, wondered why he devoted so much time to a scruffy captain who was working for a mystery client and, at best, might produce a modest commission. Dennis and I had become friends, which, of course, is almost never good for business.

The few Fishers that we did find were either out of Rich's price range, in need of complete refits or under contract. We even flew down to Jersey, in the Channel Islands, to look at an older 34 which, according to the listing sheet, was well-equipped and in good condition. After inspecting the boat, we suspected that the kindly owner, a shy, stuttering chap who desperately wanted to sell, suffered from color blindness. He had recently painted the boat himself and while the paint job was almost comically bad, the color scheme, dull brown topsides with bright yellow decks and wheelhouse, made the boat look like a giant, wrinkled beehive.

Dennis was right about the Americans; they were everywhere. It was the mid-80s and the pound sterling was losing value by the minute, especially against the U.S. dollar. We encountered Yankee sailors looking for bargain boats in every marina and heard familiar accents in the many dockside pubs.

Flying back across the Channel, the prop plane lumbered through the beginnings of what would become a Force 11 blow later that day. Looking down at the angry gray and white confusion, I realized that a stout little wheelhouse might not be a bad idea after all, even one that looked like a floating beehive. The plane hit the runway like a hungry pelican hits the water and it was a relief to stumble into the rent-a-car. By the time we reached Dennis' office, we had decided to make an offer on the boat. I was conjuring excuses for why we would not be able to send color pictures back to Rich when Dennis, who was on the line with the listing agent, mumbled that an accepted offer had been tendered just a few hours before, by a couple from Texas no less. I was desperate.

It was April 20th and we weren't close to buying a boat. We were planning to take the southern route across the North Atlantic, and ride the 'ladies' trades' from the Canaries to the Caribbean. We were racing the weather and needed to be away from England by May 1 to complete most of the crossing before the onset of hurricane season in the tropics. Dennis' wife, who eventually became a good friend, took pity on me, topped my tea as I started to pore over the sailboat listings for the umpteenth time.

"This is a nice little boat," Dennis remarked with strained enthusiasm while pulling a yellowed spec sheet from the file drawer. "It's an Alan Buchanan design, she is a well-respected boat, quite capable, you know. I don't know why she's still on the market though, might be a problem there."

The reason I liked Dennis was that he said things that other yacht brokers didn't, namely the truth, and like me, he was never going to be rich.

"What kind of boat is it?" I inquired, without shifting my glance from the brokerage ads in the latest issue of *Yachting Monthly*.

"A Neptunian 33."

"A what?"

"Neptunian, you know, Neptune, the Roman sea god," Dennis said, exasperated, and handed me the listing sheet and a few pictures.

"I know, I know, Dennis, I may be an American but I'm not that ignorant. It's just a strange name for a boat, kind of sacrilegious in a way."

I studied the pictures for a few moments. She wasn't beautiful but she wasn't bad either; in fact, she had much nicer lines than the Fishers we'd been looking at. Or maybe it was just that she actually looked like a sailboat if you used your thumb to blot out the abrupt midships pilothouse. The severe structure, resembling a World War I pillbox, struck me as an afterthought, like something added after experiencing a Force 11 blow in the Channel. At that point, I wasn't looking for beauty; I was looking for a boat to deliver.

"Dennis, this is as close to divine intervention as I'm likely to find. If she's good enough for Neptune, she's good enough for Rich. Where is this little bugger? We'll go take a look at her."

Fortunately, the boat was on the hard in a nearby boatyard in

Hamble. Three days later, after receiving pictures by courier, a complete survey and plenty of reassurance from his young captain, Rich wired over a substantial sum of money and became the somewhat proud owner of a Neptunian 33 ketch with the tongue-twisting name of BUDDUG. The Neptunian turned out to be a well-constructed, long-keeled ketch with good gear and a trusty Perkins 4108 diesel. 'Buddug' turned out to be Welsh for a flower that is always in bloom. It must have sounded better in Celtic because in midwestern American English, it sounded more like something you'd say after your team missed a crucial free throw, or the stock market collapsed, "Oh, buddug!" After the surveyor pronounced her fit for the crossing, suggesting only that we replace some of the running rigging and the prop, one frantic week later we were ready for sailing.

Rich's curiosity was killing him; he just couldn't stand the thought of buying a boat and not at least seeing it once before she set off on a 5,000-mile sea trial. At the last minute, he flew over to introduce himself to BUDDUG. Fortunately, he never completely recovered from jet lag during a whirlwind weekend visit. By the time we put him back on the plane, if he had any doubts about the boat, he was too exhausted to remember what they were. His visit did have one profound impact on the voyage. On reading the fine print of the delivery insurance policy that he arranged, I discovered that we needed a crew of three for the crossing.

There wasn't time to post signs on bulletin boards in various marinas and wait for people to call or turn up at the boat, so I made my way to a crew agency in Southampton. For a hefty fee, they gave me several names to contact. I found a pub with a quiet pay phone and went to work. On my first call I reached the father of the person I was looking for, a certain Paul Hunter, who lived in Stockton on Tees, in North Yorkshire. Paul's father was very enthusiastic and assured me that his son, of whom he was obviously quite proud, would be a terrific crew. "He'll never let you down, bet your crackers on that. Just give me the word and I'll put him on the next train to Southampton." My instincts told me that if Paul was anything like his dad, he was our man and I didn't make any more calls.

When I returned to the boat, Molly, who was stowing provisions and making an inventory of spare parts, greeted me with the interesting news that there was no way to reef the mainsail. BUD-DUG was fitted with a worm-gear roller-reefing boom, a ridiculous way of shortening sail that was popular back in the 70s. She had scoured the boat looking for the reefing handle which fit the gear. I called Dennis, who called the former owner, and eventually found out that he hadn't reefed in years and had no idea about the handle. The spar manufacturer was long out of business and an afternoon spent prowling through second-hand marine shops was fun but fruitless. I was about to design and rig a new slab-reefing system, which would have required dragging the main off to a sailmaker to fit reef points and adding several turning blocks to the boom. The marina manager suggested we call Roger Porter who lived across Southampton Water in Warsash and ran a small machine shop in his garage

Roger tapped on the hull a few hours later. He was at least 65, maybe 75. He was also completely blind. "Yes," he said, introducing himself, "I lost the last of my sight about 10 years back. That's what forced me to stop skippering the hydrofoil."

"You ran a hydrofoil?" I asked politely, wondering if the old man was senile and worrying that we were wasting more of our precious time.

"Oh, yes, the big one that ran out of Portsmouth, carried a lot of people, but after I couldn't really see anymore, I just had to give it up. You can only do so much by feel. Anyway, what can I do for you young people?"

The old man hopped aboard agilely as I explained our problem. "That's no problem, that's just a minor irritation. I can make you up a handle in a few hours. Just show me where the fitting is."

"I have already taken the dimensions of the shaft, it's . . ."

"Please son, I don't mean to be rude, just let me feel the fitting. I don't trust other people's measurements."

I led Roger to the gooseneck fitting and his fingers led him to the worm gear. "It looks like you need a square, ¾-inch shaft, maybe 8 inches long for leverage," he noted casually. "And where is the mast? We don't want to make the handle too long. Six inches should do nicely. I don't have any 316-grade stainless in the shop at the moment, but I think the 304 will do nicely. Here is my card. Come by the house tonight after dinner and pick it up. Oh, bring five pounds with you for my trouble, cheers."

That evening we found Roger's house in, as he described it, a 'working class' part of town. He led us back to his immaculate shop. "I just have to polish it up," he said, obviously wanting to show off a bit as he skillfully shined the handle on a wire wheel. I didn't blame him, for his work was superb, better than most machinists with 20/20 vision. I thanked him sincerely and insisted on giving him 10 pounds. He would not take it. Instead he gave me a spare handle, just as well made as the first. "I know you're not as clumsy as me but I have been known to drop a few things over the side. I figured a spare wouldn't cause any harm. Have a nice trip. Cheers."

Paul Hunter arrived at the boat later that evening. He was just what I expected, young (although only two years younger than me, he seemed like a kid), in great shape and incredibly excited at the prospect of sailing across the Atlantic. Although he had little sailing experience, any semblance of an interview evaporated as we struck up an immediate friendship and soon we were tipping back a few pints in the Salty Dog Pub and making plans for our departure.

The English Channel greeted us appropriately as we cleared The Needles just before dark. It was a clear, cold and blustery night with northwest winds gusting to 30 knots. The wind and tide, elements that never seem to get along, were bickering as usual and creating lumpy conditions as we skirted Portland Bill. Paul was cheery and miserably seasick. You have to admire a person who, after heaving his guts over the rail, greets you in the cockpit with a smile. I confess I was close to joining Paul at the holy rail as the reality of my task hit me like a slap in the face from a cold Channel wave. While delivering boats seemed like a logical profession for me, especially because there was nothing else that I knew how to do that actually paid, pitching about in the English Channel made me suddenly question my new career choice. My stomach was churning as I realized that I was completely responsible for Rich's chubby little boat, as well as the safety of Molly and Paul. I had sailed around Cape Horn without a trace of squeamishness, but this was different. That was an adventure, a noble expedition, while this little jaunt across the pond was nothing more than a business trip. The press didn't come down to the wharf to see us off; we were not racing history or trying to set records; we were not even part of the cruising fraternity. We were cold professionals hired to sail a boat across an ocean. It did not matter that BUDDUG was charging toward Ile d'Ouessant and the Bay of Biscay at 6.5 knots. On that chilly English night, Fort Lauderdale seemed farther away than the dim flicker of Venus descending into the western darkness.

It took me two days to remember that we had a mizzen. I had never sailed a ketch before. By the time I slipped out of the wheelhouse and cracked my head on the mizzen boom while taking a piss, we were out of the English Channel, motoring across a benign Bay of Biscay. It was hard to believe that these were the same waters that had conspired to make my life as miserable as possible two years before when we left England in late November aboard GIGI. I was feeling much better and, as we ambled across Biscay, I had reconciled my earlier misgivings. Indeed, I found a peculiar attraction to this new type of sailing, as I conjured a new vision of myself. I was a sailing mercenary. Yes, sir, I was a working sailor. I was the guy you could count on to bring your boat home, period. I was the man for the job, any sails job. It didn't matter that this was my first long-distance delivery and that I had no idea what travails loomed ahead, both on this voyage and the many others to come. I was comfortable with this new, tough-guy image. I'd gone from noble explorer to hardened gunslinger. Of course, I was just replacing one romantic scenario with another. But at sea it's vital to keep your romantic illusions intact as long as possible.

Four days out of Hamble, the wind returned and so did my sense of perspective. Rolling before the Portuguese trades, I gained respect for the ketch rig as we skipped along under jib and jigger. I also realized that while self-image might have bearing on the launching of certain projects, it has almost nothing to do with carrying them out. As much as I tried to rationalize the idea that I'd gone from explorer to gunslinger and that this was nothing more than a business trip, it just didn't wash. We all need to bolster our resolve when setting off in a new direction; yet once in tune with the rhythm of the sea, I knew this was far more than a business trip. I was in the environment that made me feel alive. I was completely at home aboard a small boat. I was so damned happy to be back where I belonged, in the realm where the flying fishes play, I didn't even care that the alternator suddenly refused to charge the batteries as we neared the Canary Islands.

Just before sunset, we sighted the towering Pico del Teide,

which looms 12,000 feet over the island of Tenerife. Early the next morning, we made landfall in San Andres, a grimy fishing harbor just north of the island's main city, Santa Cruz. In just more than 11 days, we logged 1,550 miles for a surprising average of 135 miles a day. After squeezing every fender we had between BUD-DUG's topsides and the ragged seawall, we stumbled to the nearest café for the ceremonial cold beer and first meal ashore. A delicious and heaping shellfish paella was the perfect tonic for a week and a half of boat food. After *café con leche* and a sweet *emsaimada*, I went in pursuit of an electrician.

My Spanish, which is a little better now, was dreadful then: If I wasn't ordering a beer or looking for the bathroom, I was more or less incommunicado. I finally convinced a disgruntled electrician to follow me back to the boat. After a brief inspection of the alternator and electrical system, the electrician, who was suspiciously immaculate and nattily dressed in a purple leisure suit (obviously he was on his way to a siesta rendezvous), declared with utter certainty that it was not an electrical problem but a mechanical one and that we needed to have the alternator rebuilt. This was good news. Paul and I quickly popped out the alternator and dropped it off at the local Perkins dealer.

The next morning, May 10, I cheerfully retrieved the alternator. I saw no reason why we could not be away by May 12, which would almost certainly see us across the Atlantic before the onset of hurricane season. Paul and I carefully installed the alternator and then fired up the diesel. I stared at the voltmeter with despair; the batteries were not charging. Paul put a meter directly on the batteries to confirm what we already knew, and we checked and rechecked our connections. Furious, I removed the alternator again and hurried back to the engine shop, this time with my Spanish dictionary.

"*No carga*," I shouted at the unsuspecting mechanic. "No carga, no stinking carga!"

He seemed puzzled and motioned for me to follow him into the shop. He hooked the alternator to a bench tester and turned it on. The needle shot up to 40 amps. It was charging with a vengeance. Unfortunately, the alternator wasn't the problem. I shook my head and apologized, carefully looking up each word in my dictionary. The mechanic patted me on the back and said something like, "*Tu problema no está mecánico, está eléctrico.*" My Spanish was good enough to know that I should never have trusted an electrician in a polyester leisure suit.

For the next three days a steady stream of experts were paraded on and off the boat, all suggesting a different solution to our desperate cries of *no carga*. The general consensus pointed the blame at the regulator, but four new regulators later, there was still *no carga*. Finally, working late into the evening of May 13, Paul and I, with the help of an English-speaking electrician off a Uruguayan merchant ship, began tearing the electrical system apart from top to bottom. Paul noticed a broken wire behind the key switch. After splicing the wire back together, we nervously fired up the engine, still *no carga*. "Wait," I shouted and hastily shut down the engine. I then reinstalled the old regulator and we tried again. "*Si, carga bueno.*" The entire problem had been caused by a broken wire. I didn't know whether to laugh or cry.

The next day we decided to have a final meal ashore before topping off our provisions and setting sail. We took a taxi into Santa Cruz and found a nice restaurant overlooking the harbor. We had a lovely meal, complete with wine and dessert. When the bill came, I presented my credit card. We were low on cash and I wanted to save our remaining pesetas for fuel and provisions. The waiter returned with a somber look. It seemed my credit card had expired a few weeks before. I was forced to spend a good portion of our dwindling cash reserves for lunch. Judging that fuel was more important than food, we miserly picked up a few extra items at the *mercado* and, after filling our fuel tanks to the brim, raced the fading daylight out of the harbor.

Although it is about 1,500 miles from England to the Canary Islands and another 1,000 miles or so from the Caribbean Islands north to Florida, it's the leg from the Canary Islands to the Caribbean that constitutes the real Atlantic crossing. When the last glimpse of land fades from view astern, you know that you'll have nothing but blue horizons for nearly 3,000 miles. In the days of sailing ships and before the age of political correctness, the steady northeast winds that prevail on this route came to be known as the 'ladies' trades', for they were usually well mannered and, if you avoided hurricane season, rarely reached gale force. It took five days for BUDDUG and her crew to unveil the elusive ladies' trades and when we finally found them, they were, as advertised, steady but gentle. We flew the cruising spinnaker night and day, and trimmed the mizzen primarily to keep the autopilot from working too much. After a week at sea, we had logged only 849 miles. BUD-DUG was lolling along at 5 knots.

Most sailors make this passage in the late fall and early winter. When leaving the Canary Islands, they work south as quickly as possible to pick up the easterlies. The passage is usually done around or below latitude 15 degrees north, and Barbados, the eastern-most of the Windward Islands, is the traditional landfall. In spring and summer the trades are lighter and drift a little farther north. I was hoping that we could make most of the crossing straddling the 20th parallel. This would allow for a landfall in the northern Leeward Islands. I was aiming for St. Martin, which would slice several hundred miles off the passage. We dipped down to 17 degrees and reached up to 21 degrees looking for the trades. Our second week at sea was almost a repeat of the first: The winds were gentle at best, the weather almost annoyingly fair, and the sailing too easy.

I had a nagging suspicion, however, that the Atlantic was not going to let us sneak all the way across the edge of her world without throwing a few obstacles in our path. As if to allay my fears, the tradewinds sprang to life as we began our third week at sea. BUD-DUG gamboled along at 6-plus knots and I promised the crew that if we arrived on the 20th day, we'd take a taxi to Marigot on the French side of St. Martin and have dinner at La Vie en Rose, a quaint bistro overlooking the harbor which triggered fond memories. My motivation worked. After three days of good breezes and aggressive sailing, we were only 500 miles from land. We could taste the appetizers at La Vie en Rose because at that point, even if the wind vanished, we had enough fuel to maintain good speed. A 20-day passage seemed probable.

The wind blew itself out and BUDDUG wallowed in leftover swells. Although we still had more than 50 gallons of fuel in the starboard tank, in a perverse twist of fate, the engine had developed a mysterious oil leak. In my haste to depart, I failed to purchase enough oil. There was nothing to do but whistle for wind and try not to think about the St. Emilion Bordeaux, fresh baguette, leg of lamb roasted in banana leaves and crepes suzette. On the 23rd day, the trades, which, abandoning our manners, we no longer called ladies, finally returned and we spied St. Martin from the spreaders. Doing away with my usual caution when approaching land, we kept the spinnaker flying as we skirted several shoals in the darkness before dropping the hook in Philipsburg Harbour just before midnight. So much for La Vie en Rose. We had to raid the abandon-ship bag to find anything left with which to celebrate our crossing. We toasted our achievement with a feast of stagnant tank water, the English equivalent of Spam and dry cereal with ketchup.

We purchased oil, fixed the leak and carried on to St. Thomas, 100 miles away across the Anegada Passage. Tacking through the Virgin Islands was like putting on a pair of old jeans; these were familiar and friendly waters. After another short stay, we were underway again, bound for Fort Lauderdale. Three days out, the U.S. Coast Guard came calling. We were in international waters, more than 200 miles from the nearest island. Although I offered no invitation, they boarded BUDDUG and thoroughly searched the boat. They were professional but stern-faced and I was angry and uncooperative. I have never responded well to men or women in costumes, especially when they claim authority and bring their jingoistic rules to an environment as neutral and honest as the ocean. I became indignant when the boarding officer, after failing to find any illegal substances aboard, issued me a safety violation. It seems we didn't have a proper throwing device on deck. I told the young officer that he would make a fine throwing device and, fortunately, Molly and Paul intervened before things got completely out of control.

I stewed for days over the boarding. I knew that I handled the situation poorly, but I was still angry that my own country's Coast Guard would have the audacity to presume I was running drugs. I hate drugs, not from a moral standpoint but from a navigational one. I resent that drug dealers have made those in authority suspicious of anyone who plies the ocean in a small boat.

Eight days out of St. Thomas, the ubiquitous condo towers that stand sentinel over the Florida coast decorated the horizon. I called Rich on the VHF radio and gave him an ETA for the fuel dock at the Fort Lauderdale marina. I was proud of myself, proud of Molly and Paul, and proud of little BUDDUG. As we scrubbed her decks and tidied her cabin, I felt that sense of well-being that swells your chest after a passage well done. I also began to lower

my guard, knowing that in a few hours I would hand Rich the keys
to his stout little ship, collect the balance owed me, and be on my
merry way.

Before I could even spend the money burning a hole in my
pocket, I was off and running on a series of short deliveries. I was
amazed and delighted that I was actually making a living moving
sailboats from one place to another. I felt like I was stealing. I took
a Gulfstar 37 across the Gulf of Mexico to Galveston Bay and a
Morgan 45 over to the Bahamas. I fetched an Irwin 52 in Jack-
sonville, sailed an Endeavor 40 up the East Coast from Fort Lauderdale to New York and brought a Cheoy Lee 44 home to
Annapolis from Bermuda. In what would become a common but
never easy run, I ferried a Morgan Out-Island 41 ketch down to St.
Thomas. These stout but stubby center-cockpit battleships, known
by professional skippers as Out House 41s, were still popular in the
Caribbean charter trade in those days. The 1,000-mile passage
from Florida was dead to windward and a real struggle in an OI 41.
Charter companies didn't pay very well, but for some reason I didn't
mind beating my brains to weather for 8 or 9 days at a time.

I learned more about boats during these deliveries than I cared
to know. I encountered a host of problems, from ruptured exhaust
manifolds to burst hydraulic steering lines, to blown-out sails and
cobbled-up furling systems. Although I'm anything but mechanical by nature, gradually I learned how to repair many of the diverse
components that combine to make most sailboats symphonies of
chaos. More importantly, I trusted in my long-held motto: If
something breaks, figure out why you never really needed it in the
first place and get on with the voyage. I do, however, have a persistent nature and I almost always turned up when I said I would,
with few if any complaints. This attitude, along with the fact that I
was a good celestial navigator in those pre-GPS days, made me a
busy delivery skipper.

Molly was much less smitten with this vagrant way of life and
frustrated by the things we didn't have. The fact that we had cheap,
inflatable furniture in our tiny apartment seemed to bother her the
most. It seemed quite practical to me. We could move in 15 minutes. I loved having few possessions, the less I had the better I felt.
I had my sextant, my sailing gear and my books; I didn't need anything else. Molly and I were growing apart as I made more and

more deliveries on my own. However, when we received an intriguing letter from my mother, even Molly was happy that all we had to do was deflate the furniture, haul the books to my sister's garage, and hop on a plane.

Feeling smug after another delivery is completed.

My mother and her mate Tim MacTaggart were sailing around the world in her 38-foot Jeanneau sloop EPOCH. Mom and Tim, both in their early 60s, had left Fort Lauderdale three years before and were currently in Sri Lanka. Their 20,000-mile odyssey had taken them across the South Pacific and most of the way across the Indian Ocean. However, Mom wasn't feeling well and the next leg, a 5,000-mile passage across the Arabian Sea and up the Red Sea to the Mediterranean, promised to be challenging. Thoughts of tropical cyclones in the Arabian Sea, a likely beat up the reef-edged Red Sea, and potential Middle East political hassles helped Mom decide that she'd had enough of four hours on and four hours off. She also knew that I would be fascinated sailing in this distant corner of the world and she looked forward to sharing her adventure with me. She wrote asking if Molly and I would join them in Sri Lanka and help sail EPOCH to Cyprus. How can you say no to your mother?

The wilting languorous heat 300 miles above the Equator made autumn in Fort Lauderdale seem downright temperate. The flight, via Frankfurt, Karachi and Bombay, was endless as Sri Lanka is about as far as you can fly from Miami in one direction before you start getting closer again. Completely exhausted, we joined Mom and Tim aboard EPOCH in the southern port city of Galle. I was nervous about our impending voyage. My mother and I are very much alike, and we are the best of friends. We have the type of relationship that does not judge behavior; whatever she does is okay and she gives me the same latitude. Although we have had titanic arguments, in the end, we always reach a mutual consensus. We know the answers to the world's ills, and how to preserve our special friendship. I have fathomless respect for her and was damned proud that she had sailed halfway around the world and boorishly proclaimed her accomplishments to anyone willing to listen.

Unfortunately, I never gave Tim the credit he deserved. I always spoke of "my mother's voyage." I resented Tim, who was a kind, generous man and like my mother and myself, simply had a keen desire to explore the world by sailboat. Although Tim never acted in a paternal manner, he couldn't win because his very presence inspired comparisons with my father. I knew that it was going to be hard to keep my feelings under wraps in a 38-foot world, but I promised myself I would try.

We tarried in the former British colony of Ceylon for almost a month, awaiting the arrival of the tardy northeast monsoon and favorable sailing conditions. The island nation of Sri Lanka is shaped like a teardrop that has fallen from the face of India and with the continued trouble between Hindu separatists in the north and the island's primarily Buddhist population in the south, the shape seems sadly symbolic. Sinbad and his fellow Arab sea-traders called the island Serendip, which translates into the English word serendipity, an apt description.

I was enchanted and at times overwhelmed as Sri Lanka assaulted my bland western senses. Lumbering ox carts, creaking rickshaws, entire families riding and laughing on one bicycle, swaying snake charmers and chanting monks created early morning cacophony. The warm sea breeze would carry the scent of jasmine as it wafted over land. The same capricious wind might also convey the sickly stench of open sewers and droppings from cows and goats that roamed the streets. My eyes beheld a bewildering array of colors: vivid saris draped around dark, sensuous women; almond-eyed monks in saffron robes; and bizarre batik creatures of every shade glaring at me from behind shop windows. Even a simple bowl of rice was likely to make my eyes water and I came to admire the flavor of spices I'd never even heard of a few weeks before.

From sailing with fishermen in local boats called *oruwas*, to climbing overgrown archaeological ruins that rival anything in Greece and Rome, to stumbling across a herd of wild elephants, I fell under the spell of Serendip. I understood why Sri Lanka has inspired so many writers, from Chekhov and Kazantzakis, to Paul Bowles and Arthur Clarke. I wrote in my journal that one day I would return to Sri Lanka, and I will. However, it was time to leave as we had run out of patience with the weather. Ignoring a foreboding sky and stiff northwest headwinds, we set sail for Cochin, India, on the Malabar coast. According to the pilot charts, November was the tail end of the Indian Ocean cyclone season and the odds of encountering a storm were remote. Naturally, EPOCH and her crew personally bid farewell to the last cyclone of the season as torrential rains and 40-knot winds made the 300-mile passage up to Cochin wet and miserable.

Cochin, dubbed by sanguine Indian tourist officials as the 'Venice of India', was our first stop on a course that roughly paral-

Sailing an *Oruwa*, a native boat, in Sri Lanka, while delivering EPOCH.

leled the Arab trading routes of the Middle Ages. In Cochin, sail was alive and well as large dhows, sleek *bedans*, double-ended booms and swift sailing canoes plied the many waterways. If you blotted out the ugly concrete buildings in the background, the exotic assortment of lateen rigs with patchwork sails could carry you back to the days of the Arabian Nights. I wonder, however, if Sinbad was as frustrated as we were by the form-filling, carbon-paper-carrying officials who have nothing better to do than take up your time, in triplicate, of course. Officialdom is overwhelming in India as customs and immigration offices provide layers of meaningless jobs for far too many people. It took us two days to clear in and two more to clear out.

The mere thought of dealing with more uniformed paper-pushers persuaded us to skip other Malabar ports and we continued north to Bombay. We followed a handsome dhow, at least 80 feet long, into Bombay's wide, natural harbor and anchored in the shadow of the Gateway to India. This ostentatious arch, built by the British, stands as a constant reminder of India's less than noble colonial past.

Everyone knows that Bombay is a sprawling, grossly overpopulated, filthy city. It is also a vibrant business center and the cultural showcase of India. Bombay forces you to address your feelings

We follow a classic dhow into Bombay Harbor.

about this contrasting country of excesses. For me, I found it difficult to divert my glance from the maimed and destitute; they are everywhere. As more and more rural Indians pour into Bombay with hopes of finding work, more and more people join the hordes already living, and dying, on the streets. A sailboat with her annoying idiosyncrasies insists that you participate in a foreign society with your eyes wide open, and to a degree that the average traveler never experiences. Aside from clearing customs in commercial harbors, not in air-conditioned airports, the simple act of provisioning can be most enlightening. You haggle at the market and butcher shop, trying to ignore the flies hovering over the hunks of raw meat and the cockroaches in the banana stalls. You scour back alleys in search of esoteric fittings. In Bombay, we miraculously found an antenna for the SatNav in a yacht electronics shop that also did dry cleaning and brokered prostitutes. When it came time to top our water tanks, we had to mobilize about 20 young men for a six-block bucket brigade.

Bombay was swallowed up in its own pollution before we were five miles offshore. It was two days before Christmas and we were all happy to be back at sea. Even EPOCH seemed spacious after the constant crowds of India—or maybe it was just the promise of lovely empty horizons looming ahead. We were bound for Aden, in the

People's Democratic Republic of Yemen, 1,700 miles across the Arabian Sea. Unhappily, after Christmas it was obvious that Mom was seriously ill. She was not her buoyant, annoyingly optimistic self. It seems the windy crossing from Australia to Sri Lanka months before had taken its toll and she was calling on hidden reserves of strength just to keep going. During our stay in India we were all sick but the 'Bombay blues' hit her the hardest. We decided to detour to Raysut in Oman. Mom needed medical attention.

We reached Raysut on New Year's eve and after polishing off all our contraband booze (alcohol is not permitted in Oman), we collapsed into bed long before 1986 officially arrived. The next morning Mom was escorted by the police to the hospital. Yachts were not encouraged to visit Oman and anytime we went ashore, we had a friendly police escort. We were treated well, as long as we accepted the fact that a policeman would accompany us everywhere we went. The hospital, like most of the buildings in nearby Salalah, was brand new, squeaky clean and modern. Sultan Qaboos, who had deposed his father 15 years before, was using his vast oil revenues to transform his country from an isolated land of Bedouins into a modern state. The transition was curious to observe, as Mercedes dueled with camels on newly paved highways.

Mom was X-rayed from every angle as her American-trained doctor thoroughly examined her. The diagnosis was as clear as the empty desert sky: She had severe bronchial pneumonia. The doctor urged her to fly home and reluctantly, she followed his orders. She was distraught at leaving EPOCH, but there was no other safe option. After Mom departed, the voyage assumed a true delivery air and urgency suited us all. We had a job to do: sail EPOCH to the Mediterranean. The sooner we put the volatile Middle East behind us, the better. On January 9, we cleared out of Oman and once again set sail for Aden.

We were dusted by a *khamsin*, the local name for a northerly gale, that peppered the decks with sand. Five days out of Raysut, the sky cleared and the dramatic headland of Jabal Shamshan lay abeam, half shaded by the early morning sun. The sheer rock face, nearly 2,000 feet high, marks the southern end of a narrow, twisting peninsula that shelters the port of Aden from relentless monsoon winds. I stared transfixed at a winding footpath leading into the depths of the desolate landscape. I felt a strange kinship with the invisible Bedouin. Like me, a restless traveler, he crosses oceans of sand, in search of what, a rare oasis? I cross oceans of bluewater, in search of what, serendipity? My dreaming was shattered when the gunboat fired at us.

Boom! A red tracer shell whizzed overhead and hit the water about 200 yards behind EPOCH. A stealthy, gray gunboat, ahead and offshore, was firing at us! Boom! Another shell groaned as it passed 100 feet above the mast. Boom! A red tracer skipped perilously close astern. What in the hell was going on? I dashed below and screamed MAYDAY into the VHF radio. Nobody responded.

Aden is the capital of what was then the People's Democratic Republic of Yemen, a Marxist state formerly called South Yemen. Strategically located 90 miles east of the Straits of Bab el Mandeb, Aden provided the Soviet navy with a handy perch to monitor the traffic that flows in and out of the Red Sea. According to the yachtie pipeline, the People's Democratic Republic of Yemen, although communist, was a safe waypoint for boats headed toward the Red Sea. In fact, before we were fired upon, Molly joked that she was glad the People's Democratic Republic of Yemen was communist because she had a thirst for a cold beer and no patience with teetotaling Moslems.

Crouched low in the cockpit, Tim hit the throttle and we closed the coast. Forward, toward Aden's inner harbor, was the only logical course because the gunboat had fired deliberately behind us—at least we hoped that was deliberate. We reasoned that we had somehow accidentally sailed into an artillery range, although there was no mention of it on the chart. The gunboat continued sporadic firing, but well astern, and gradually we started breathing again. Hurrying toward the inner harbor, we even managed to chuckle at our apparent naiveté. Of course, we couldn't see the Soviet tanks and AK 47-toting foot soldiers maneuvering for position on the streets of Aden.

"This must be a serious military exercise," Tim said in his most convincing manner. "They obviously were not trying to hit us or they could have blown us out of the water."

"I guess that's reassuring, and it makes sense," I added, "but it sure seems like a dangerous way to warn somebody."

Molly wondered why nobody responded to our MAYDAY. "The military must have ordered radio silence for the exercise,"

Tim suggested, and I quipped, "You know, the boys probably have some new toys from Moscow and want to show them off."

The words were no sooner out of my mouth when Boom! Boom! Boom! powerful blasts exploded from the mountainside above us. A heavy artillery gun was launching volleys from a pill-box, over our mast, out toward the gunboats.

"This is crazy." Molly cried. "This is more than an exercise."

"Of course it's an exercise." I insisted, "Even Arabs are better shots than that."

By this time we could see the breakwaters protecting the inner harbor. We tried unsuccessfully to tune in the BBC on the short-wave radio. Suddenly, a massive explosion shook the atmosphere and a few seconds later a rocket salvo hit the water just, and I mean just, outside the inner harbor. EPOCH shuddered. We were stunned and silent. Then a rusty gunboat came charging out of the harbor, heading directly toward us. Several armed men in tattered uniforms lined the bridge. As the gunboat neared EPOCH, they must have thought us utterly mad as we waved politely and asked, "What's going on?"

The bearded leader spoke little English but made his point clearly. Pointing to a nearby bay, just outside the harbor, he screamed, "There, there, NOW!" With a cannon trained amidships and several rifles aimed at our heads, no explanation was needed. Tim swung EPOCH about and we dutifully anchored just east of Cape Iarshain, directly opposite the inner harbor. We didn't know it at the time, but we had the best seat in the house to observe what would soon become a full-scale civil war.

The surroundings ashore were eerie, the buildings were strangely deserted, windows were shattered and everything was en-compassed by barbed wire. Incredulously, Tim and I clung to our belief—or maybe it was a desperate hope—that this was still some type of military exercise, albeit an extremely realistic one. I poured a round of stiff drinks to settle our nerves and kept my eyes glued to the gun emplacements dotting the hillside. Suddenly, a MIG 21 fighter appeared out of nowhere, just a flash across the sky. Seconds later a tower of black smoke spiraled skywards about a half mile from where we lay anchored. Then we heard small arms fire, spo-radic, rat-tat-tat, rat-tat-tat echoed from the shoreline 100 yards away. More heavy artillery erupted from the hillside. Each time a shell hit the water, EPOCH reverberated with such force that I feared the keelbolts might sheer off. Then another MIG left a trail of fire on the nearby streets. This was much more than a military exercise as the BBC 1500 news report finally confirmed.

Heavy fighting continues in Aden, the capital of the People's Democratic Republic of Yemen. A radical Marxist faction is attempting to overthrow the moderate Marxist regime of President Ali Nasser Muhammad. The situation is confused and there are contradicting reports of intense fighting. The government radio station remains silent for the second day. One confirmed report relays that several merchant ships have been damaged and small boats have been sunk.

We had sailed right into the middle of a coup d'état. I felt a strange combination of fear, anger and stupidity, knowing that we could have skirted the entire melee if we had just listened to the radio or realized that the first gunboat had been trying to warn us. Now we were trapped. At least we were not in the inner harbor. The eight sailboats that we could see in the harbor, sandwiched directly between the warring factions, were in the worst possible position. We were a quarter mile to the east. The three of us were terrified and extremely confused. Who was fighting whom? Why did the gunboat intercept us and force us into this bay? It seemed like the navy and the air force were trying to take out the army positions, but the 1600 and 1700 BBC reports were sketchy at best. At 1800, however, the BBC reported that the situation was escalating and the British were making plans to evacuate their embassy. More disturbing was the news that the Soviets were also clearing out.

The sun was setting: It was time for a decision. I was for leaving, at once, at all costs. Tim insisted that we stay put, arguing that it was too dangerous. "We might be hit by a stray shell, or maybe by a deliberate one. Also," he said, "they saw our flag, they know we're Americans. They might make good use of three hostages."

I forcefully disagreed. "We have to move now while we still can. If the gunboats were intent on blowing us to smithereens, they would have done so by now. We'll just have to take our chances and hope like hell that the shore guns don't fire on us." Molly was unsure but leaned toward moving. The minutes dragged on, each second seemed like an eternity and still no decision was made. This was the very situation I dreaded: You can't have two captains on the same boat. Tim and I had done well not stepping on each other's turf. I was the navigator and he made the sailing decisions. Now, however, our very survival depended on a bold course of action. Luckily, the choice became obvious when we noticed a Soviet ship steam out of the harbor. Another ship followed and then another; it was an exodus of merchant ships. The VHF came alive as frantic skippers discussed emergency procedures, everyone agreed that they had to leave at once.

I knew that this convoy of ships was our best chance for escape. I told Tim to fire up the engine and I dashed forward and hauled up the anchor, like a super human, hand-over-hand windlass. Twilight was waning as we made our way toward the fleeing ships. Six knots never seemed slower as we nervously watched the gunboats form a blockade. Would they let us through? Yes! The first ships cleared the gunboats. We did our best to keep up but fell farther and farther behind the ships. "A lot of eyes are on us right now," Tim mumbled from the helm. "Ya, and a lot of guns are aimed at us too," I added. Our spirits soared as we watched the ships harmlessly pass the ring of gunboats. Finally, it was our turn. Suddenly, one of the gunboats broke rank and came charging toward us. It slowed as it approached and then came to stop, about 50 yards off our port beam. A soldier left the bridge and walked slowly to the evil turret on the bow. Time stood still. The turret turned toward us. He was going to blow us into oblivion. We were defenseless. I felt rage melt into utter despair. As West Indian sailors say when they are certain to pile up on the rocks, "I could smell the flowers on my grave site." No, the turret turned away and the gunboat steamed off. The bastards were toying with us.

Our escape from Aden was made just in time. Later, we would hear firsthand of the terrors that took place in the city. We set a course for Djibouti, a 'friendly country' carved out of Ethiopia on the horn of Africa. Oh, yes, we also tuned in the BBC every hour.

The civil war in the People's Democratic Republic of Yemen was strictly an internal affair and shrouded in mystery. Three weeks after the fighting broke out, *Time* magazine reported, "dismayingly little was yet known about what was happening inside the People's Democratic Republic of Yemen." We read some reports that as many as 12,000 people perished in the madness. Trevor Robertson, who abandoned his yacht SALVATION JANE in the inner harbor, stayed aboard EPOCH in Djibouti and told a chilling tale. When the fighting broke out, the crews of the eight yachts in the harbor were just as confused as we had been. Even when they suspected a dangerous situation was brewing, they were reluctant to leave because the Aden authorities retained their boat papers and passports. However, by noon on January 14, the day we arrived, they realized the situation was indeed serious. Several yachts had been strafed and hit by shrapnel. One yacht, ironically an English ketch named INNOCENT BYSTANDER, was deliberately sunk when she tried to leave. Robertson explained that the crews of the remaining yachts knew their only chance for survival was to get aboard one of the merchant ships. The Soviet skipper of the ship that began the exodus announced on the radio that he was going to open his cargo door for 10 minutes. Each yacht crew had to make the painful decision to abandon their boat and then undertake a perilous dinghy ride to the ship. The Soviet skipper dropped the crews off in Djibouti and there they remained, wondering and hoping that when the fighting stopped, their boats might still be afloat in Aden's inner harbor.

We stayed in Djibouti just long enough to calm our nerves and let all concerned know that we were safe and sound. We were determined to negotiate the Straits of Bab el Mandeb as soon as possible, before the fighting spread out of Aden, and slipped through the straits under a cover of darkness and fog. The vaunted Red Sea passage loomed decidedly anticlimactic. Obstacles like strong headwinds and poorly charted reefs seemed like kid's stuff compared to MIGs and rocket salvos.

*   *   *

It was Super Bowl Sunday and Lesa and I had wagered a romantic dinner on the outcome. She picked the Redskins and I, ever the optimist, went with the Bills. An ocean-going tug hauling a heavily laden barge well astern hove into view off the starboard quarter. A quick call on the VHF revealed that I'd be buying dinner as the poor old Bills had failed again in the big game. Lesa wasn't ready to gloat just yet. Her mind was still back in Aden, amid the mayhem of a city falling to pieces and a sailboat crew barely escaping with their lives. My unusually serious tale had left us both feeling somber, stealing some of the magic of our dream to sail to far-off places together. There were risks involved. The thugs back in Boca Chica didn't seem that bad all of a sudden.

"I can't believe you kept sailing toward Aden when they started shooting at you."

"I know it seems hard to believe but we just never dreamed it was a hostile situation. Talk about naive, but that's the way it was."

"Is there more to the story with Tim? You seemed reluctant to go into it. Did you guys have a blowout?"

"Yes."

"Was it ugly?"

"Yes, and it still troubles me. It happened in Djibouti, and we got past it."

I changed the subject, "We'll need to reef the main pretty soon. It's starting to blow pretty good."

Lesa dropped below and I heard her talking to the tug captain on the VHF. Back in the cockpit, I asked why she called him back.

"Oh," she said laughing, "I just wanted to make sure there wasn't a war brewing in the Turks and Caicos."

CHAPTER 5

A
Waterfront
Office

Voyaging beyond the horizon in a small vessel is knowing re-
moval from all the superfluous vexations and tribulations
which have brought modern man to a platform upon which he
stands naked and alone in his secret terror, not quite sure
whether he is rich or poor, or young or old, inspired or de-
spairing, or what his sale price should be.

ERNEST GANN, Song of the Sirens

EVENTUALLY, I FOUND my way back to Fort Lauderdale, via
Cyprus, the south coast of England and Annapolis. We left
EPOCH in Cyprus, a delivery to the orient fell through in
Southampton, and sponsorship for an Arctic sailing expedition collapsed at the last moment in Annapolis. Although there was nothing tangible in Fort Lauderdale, no family demanding my presence,
no property needing my attention, I always ended up there. It had
become, for better and worse, my spiritual base, as well as the one
place where I knew I could drum up work quickly. And while I
joked to my out-of-town friends that there was more culture in yo-
gurt than in Fort Lauderdale, the truth is, I liked the place then
and I like it even more now.

It is a crossroads for mariners, and whether sipping coffee in a
street-side café on Las Olas Boulevard or pouring over charts and
guidebooks in Bluewater Books & Charts, it is not uncommon to
hear conversations in German, Swedish, Spanish and Italian. It is

not unusual to stumble across a friend in a chandlery that you last saw in Panama, Antigua or Majorca.

Most importantly, Fort Lauderdale thrives on its transitory nature. You can leave for a month, a year, three years, and come back, print business cards proclaiming "in business since last week" and be off and running, promoting a new scheme. It is a town of fly-by-night operators and unpredictable heavy-hitters. The shaggy, bearded guy wearing a tank top and flip-flops and flirting with the waitress at the table next to you might have just signed a check for a million-dollar yacht, or—and this is the beauty of the place—he might sell newspapers on the corner of Federal Highway and Broward Boulevard.

It is also a natural home port for a sailboat-delivery skipper; sooner or later all boats seem to pass through Fort Lauderdale. In one of those impossible promises, the kind that are just what somebody wants to hear but are guaranteed to be broken, I had given Molly my word that I would spend more time in Fort Lauderdale. I assured her that I would look for short, local deliveries and concentrate on my freelance writing. However, I had few illusions about my writing. The royalties pouring in from my recently published book about the Cape Horn voyage wouldn't have paid the dockage for the boat I was dreaming about buying. And although I was selling articles to the sailing magazines with some regularity, my writing was more about passion than profit.

In an honest attempt to spend more nights in my own bed, I forged a close relationship with one of the busiest sailboat brokerages in town. I did most of the sea trials and short deliveries for Moss Yachts, which was located on the Intracoastal Waterway and managed by my pal and Cape Horn partner Ty Techera. Ty, who at one time owned a couple of industrial companies in Detroit, abandoned both his commercial enterprises and an unhappy marriage and ran away to sea. Ty took to bluewater sailing like a drunk takes to a bottle of cheap booze: He couldn't get enough as he logged thousands of miles aboard GIGI, his Contessa 32 sloop. I was his sailing mentor and he often chided me that I was responsible for ruining his life. After our little jaunt from Rio de Janeiro to Valparaiso, he made a series of impressive singlehanded voyages, including another Cape Horn rounding. Gradually, he underwent a metamorphosis. His sense of urgency was undermined—sailing will do that—and his priorities were altered. When he finally washed ashore, he followed my lead and made his way to Fort Lauderdale. To occupy his time, he started selling boats. Ty is one of those people who simply does not know how not to make money; and his combination of sailing experience, financial savvy, and the ability to sell molas to the Kuna Indians made him an excellent yacht broker. In spite of himself, he was soon running the show at Moss Yachts.

Ty and I spent many afternoons hunched over the outdoor bar at the Marina Inn, discussing, among other things, a subject I always tried to avoid, my finances.

"John, I know that money isn't as important as I once thought, but you could be making a lot more money by selling boats instead of sailing them. I'm not talking about a career. Hell no. This would be a miserable career. Just give it a year or two. Then you can buy your own boat, take off and write that novel you keep talking about."

"Ty, I don't want to sell boats."

"What does Molly want?"

"She wants me to be happy."

Ty rolled his eyes, as though he knew something I didn't. I didn't want to sell boats, I loved every aspect of being a delivery skipper and the thought of sitting behind a desk, drinking stale coffee all day and lying about boats, was not at all appealing. That was not the kind of waterfront office I wanted. In fact, I was struggling just trying to stay close to home. I was itching to sail to the other side of an ocean, any ocean. The deck of a pitching sailboat, one a long way from land: Now that was my idea of a waterfront office. I tried to change the subject but Ty barged ahead.

"I have an idea, we'll work together. I will do the financial stuff, you know the contracts and the negotiations, and you will be, how should I say it, the sailing adviser. People trust you, you're not jaded yet and, besides, you know more about boats than anybody in this town. We'll sell people the right boat, at the right price. We'll be an unbeatable combination."

Ty saw the desolate expression on my face. "Hey, we'll just be helping people launch their dreams. You don't have to surrender

your idealism all at once, and you will finally make some real
money."

"Why are you doing this, Ty?"

"For two reasons. It makes sense to take advantage of each
other's skills and also, I think it's time you learned something
about money."

"So I guess it's time for me to become jaded?"

Reluctantly, and on a limited basis, I agreed to Ty's offer to
co-broker boats. He had thrown many opportunities my way
over the years and I felt like it was my turn to respond. I owed
him something; exactly what, I couldn't say, maybe a simple debt
of friendship. Not surprisingly, Ty was right; we were an excellent team. I would show boats to clients, pointing out what I
liked, what I didn't like and, much to their surprise, what I
hated. Ty would hammer the price down while I conducted the
sea trial and closely monitored the survey. In the end, our clients
were invariably pleased, although I was never quite comfortable
with the vice grip that Ty had to apply to finally extract the
money and close every deal. With the brokerage income com-
plementing my still-busy delivery schedule, I was making money
for the first time in my life—and I was miserable. I could feel the
real world clamping down on me. I had nightmares about buying a house in the suburbs, it had a circular driveway and a white
picket fence. I had car payments, the IRS knew my name and I
could feel a shoreside paunch taking root around my middle.
After six months, I was thoroughly jaded. It was time to come
about.

Perched on familiar stools at the Marina Inn bar, I was searching for a delicate way of explaining to Ty, who seemed unusually
serious, that I'd had enough and was going to accept an offer to
deliver a new Moody 42 from England to Florida. I knew full well
that a long-distance delivery was the tonic I needed, and would put
an end to my half-hearted foray into the world of real employment.
To my surprise, Ty jumped in first.

"John," he said in a quiet, earnest voice. "I can't take this bullshit anymore. In the end, this business is just like any other business; it always boils down to money."

We had recently lost a deal when a buyer went behind our
backs and bought the boat directly from the seller.

"You know that CT 65 deal I just put together?"

"Sure, Bob Godfrey's boat."

"Right, well Bob wants me to sail across the Atlantic with him and I'm going to take him up on his offer. I'm going to bag Moss Yachts, somebody else can run it."

"You're kidding?"

"No, I'm serious."

"That's fantastic. Come on, I'll buy you another beer, then let's go quit together."

Unlike other delivery skippers, I have never objected to having the owner aboard. In fact, owners of sailboats I've delivered are well represented on the short list of my best friends. The original plan was for Molly and me and my dear friend Jean-Louis Dulaar to pick up the boat at Moody's yard and sail back via the Azores and Bermuda. It had taken more of a con job than usual to convince Molly to come along, especially because at the quasi-last moment, the owner decided to accompany us on the voyage. Although I like and have great respect for Art, the owner, he is definitely not on the short list mentioned above.

Art is the only person I have ever known to talk the entire flight across the Atlantic. I mean, every waking second was filled with chatter and by the time the 747 touched down at Gatwick, I was wondering how I could possibly survive a month of face-to-face communication. The crossing was shaping up as a classic delivery; we were in a hurry. Once again, we were racing the onset of the Atlantic hurricane season. Also, Art sorely missed Mary, his devoted wife of many years. Separated by an ocean, he was depressed, and I knew that to bolster his resolve we needed to get underway quickly. We arrived in Swanwick, familiar turf along the Hamble River, midmorning on June 8, and by the afternoon of June 11 we were underway. It is difficult for even the most experienced sailors to understand how a delivery crew can literally toss their gear aboard a boat they've never seen before and, in many cases, make sail for a long voyage the same day. I must admit, I'm not sure how I do it sometimes. It requires a mixture of knowing how to quickly and accurately size up a boat, and having an audacious trust in fate. There is, however, another prime motivating factor for hasty departures: profit. Once you cast off, you can't spend any more money. Although my personal financial statement might suggest that the delivery business is a form of social charity, it is, at least in theory, a for-profit enterprise.

Unfortunately, Jean-Louis Dulaar was delayed in Paris and had to make arrangements to catch up with us in the Azores. Jean-Louis, an artist, was having a solo exhibition of huge canvasses he had painted in my garage back in Florida. Ty had sold Jean-Louis a boat and I had taught him to sail. We had become fast friends. He was enchanted by the blue of the Gulf Stream, the mighty current that sweeps north just off the Florida coast. He wanted to capture the various shades of blue and came up with a novel approach. First, he purchased several 8 by 8-foot canvasses, heavy duty stuff used for awnings. Then, because he wanted the canvas "to understand" the blue, we towed them behind his boat back and forth in the current. After hosing them off, he painted them with a whisk broom and two-part marine epoxy paint. The result was an explosion of blues. A close inspection revealed a nude within each painting as well as the latitude and longitude of the Gulf Stream off Fort Lauderdale. For his exhibition, the canvasses were strung on a steel cable beneath the Eiffel Tower, of all places. The exhibition was a great success and extended for an extra week. Jean-Louis assured me, however, that he would meet us in Horta.

That we were headed for the Azores at all was unusual, considering we were westbound across the Atlantic. However, it was mid-June, too late for the southern tradewind route that we steered in BUDDUG and GIGI, so we opted for the most direct route to Florida. The only problem with this route planning was that it promised 4,000 miles of headwinds. While beating for days on end is never much fun, at least EXCALIBUR was well suited for a windward slog across the pond. Bill Dixon's design, featuring a center cockpit and spacious interior, cleverly masked a modern hull shape. At just over 14,000 pounds, the 42's displacement was on the light side of moderate and the underbody featured flat ends, a fin keel, and a skeg-hung rudder. The powerful sloop rig had inboard stays for tight sheeting angles. Art had specified two options that promised to make the crossing more enlightening. He chose an internal furling mast and mainsail system, and also convinced Moody's to build a special centerboard edition. The furling mainsail made sense. Although in great shape, Art was 68 and he and Mary usually sailed alone. Handling a conventional main, even with lazy jacks, was a tall order as the 42's stick was more that 60 feet above the waterline. The centerboard was more a function of geography than design preference. Art's home in central Florida was on a shallow canal and he insisted that the boat be moored in his backyard. Moody, to their credit, altered the tooling to accommodate this, as the Brits would say, "typical American request." Unfortunately, they didn't do a very good job of supporting the expanded keel section the centerboard demanded.

We beat across the Solent until we skirted the punts moored in Yarmouth Roads, just off the Isle of Wight. Coming about, we rode an ebbing current through The Needles and entered the English Channel. Earlier, in the congested Southampton waters, the Perkins diesel had mysteriously stopped and I had to frantically bleed it with the Cowes ferry bearing down on us. We made quick work of the surprisingly benign Channel and after two 150-mile days, we skirted Ile d'Ouessant and entered the Bay of Biscay. Art was a fine sailor and this was his 11th EXCALIBUR. It was a pleasure to sail with an owner who worked his boat hard, extracting every ounce of speed and only resorting to the iron jenny when the wind vanished. He had spent years racing a variety of boats up and down the East Coast and he taught this young skipper several new wrinkles.

The three of us worked out a nice rhythm and, as so often happens, Art relaxed once the bluffs and rolling hills of Dartmoor, our last glimpse of land, faded from view. I realized that his incessant chatter was a case of nerves; this voyage was a momentous event in his life, the capstone of decades of sailing, and also the first time he had been away from Mary for an extended period of time. I found myself admiring his pluck. At an age when many people are more concerned about what's being served at the early bird special at Morrison's Cafeteria, Art had made his way to England to buy a boat, and now he was sailing her home.

And we were sailing, blasting along at 8 knots on a close reach. We were into our third night when EXCALIBUR suddenly veered off course, lurched unsteadily before the wind and then gybed hard over. Molly was on watch and as I struggled into my foulweather gear and joined her on deck, she was frantically turning the wheel. Crash, there was nothing she could do to prevent another gybe. We had lost steering. I quickly furled the mainsail and as the headwind backed, we lay hove to. Molly explained that she had taken EX-CALIBUR off autopilot and was enjoying great sailing before the wheel went slack in her hands.

The southwest wind was rising; it was an ugly, rainy night, just the kind of night you don't want to lose steering. I made my way aft and hurriedly tossed bags of gear from the jam-packed lazarette. When I finally reached the rudder quadrant, I noticed that one of the steering cables had sheared a swaged end fitting. EXCALIBUR was bucking about in the 6- to 8-foot seas and the quadrant was slamming from side to side. Fixing the cable was not a difficult chore in calm weather; however in those conditions, it was a dangerous assignment. Still, we needed steering and I was reluctant to rig the emergency tiller, which previous experience had taught me would be an exercise in futility. Then I noticed the linear arm of the autopilot drive unit. Of course, the autopilot was connected directly to the quadrant, completely bypassing the cable steering system.

"Hey Molly," I shouted, "let the jib go, bring it around, crank it in and after we start moving, turn on the autopilot." Molly trimmed the sheet as EXCALIBUR gained way, right on course with the Auhohelm 6000 firmly in control. We rolled out about half the mainsail and conservatively sailed through the night and all the next day. Ironically, we had our best 24-hour run of the entire passage, 180 miles, without steering. Finally, the wind moderated enough for me to tighten a bulldog clamp around the errant cable and reconnect the steering system.

Art was in good cheer as we neared the Azores and broke out his secret stash of single malt Scotch to celebrate our successful repair and steady progress. He had discovered *Famous Grouse* on his first trip to England and purchased two bottles for the passage. He had politely requested that we steer clear of his prized Scotch, which was easy for Molly and me because neither one of us drank much at sea anyway, and especially not Scotch. Art sniffed his stainless chalice, toasted our voyage, and took a sip. In what would become his standard refrain, he closed his eyes and exclaimed, "Ah, the nectar of the gods."

An interesting star sight, utilizing Arcturus, Venus and the North Star, revealed that, after nine days, we were only 150 miles from Horta. In a lucky, but sage-sounding prediction, I told Art, who had the 2300-to-0200 watch, to look for the lights of Terceira, the eastern-most island, around midnight. Miraculously, right at midnight, or so he told me, the red glow of an aero beacon loomed into view. To Art this feat rivaled Eratosthenes calculating the circumference of the Earth in 235 BC and, with the SatNav constantly acting up, cemented my reputation as some kind of navigational wizard. We sailed through the night but the wind died in the morning. We motored between the rugged islands of São Jorge and aptly named Pico. On the western end of Pico, an improbable peak, rising all at once from sea level to nearly 8,000 feet, disappears in the low clouds until, in Disneyesque fashion, the pointy summit reappears just above the clouds and points the way to Horta on the island of Faial. Jean-Louis, who had been watching our approach from a seaside café, was there to catch our lines as we eased alongside the customs quay just before dark. To Art's complete horror, so was his girlfriend.

We had barely exchanged greetings before both Art and Jean-Louis tried to get me alone. "She's not coming," Art insisted. "I'm not going to have some strange woman on my boat."

"Relax, Art." I said. "Let's find out what his intentions are before you get all worked up. Besides, there is plenty of room aboard."

"If she comes, I'm leaving."

While Art stewed in the aft cabin, and Molly and Laurence chatted on deck, Jean-Louis and I escaped to the marina café.

"Ah, Kretschmer, it's good to see you. How was the passage with the old man?"

Jean-Louis and Art had met briefly in Florida and they didn't like each other very much. Art had the distressingly common prejudice many men of his age have against the French, as though Jean-Louis, who was my age, had anything to do with the Vichy government. And Jean-Louis was utterly disgusted every time Art mistakenly called him Jean-Pierre.

"It was okay, Jean-Pierre. Art's a pretty good shipmate."

Jean-Louis laughed, "And the boat, she's okay?"

"Yes, fine, good really, she pounds on the wind and has too much freeboard, but she is fast."

After an awkward moment of silence, I got to the point. "Dulaar, what's with the girl? What is her name, Laurence? She seems nice."

Jean-Louis, shook his head, "What can I do, she is in love!"

"And you, are you in love?"

"No."

"Is she planning on sailing with us?"

"I think she is." Jean-Louis squirmed in his chair. "You see, Kretschmer, she bought one of my paintings, we had dinner, I mentioned the voyage and, well, now she is here too."

"When did you meet her?"

"Four days ago."

"Do you want her to sail with us? Art is dead set against it."

"Why does he care, what is his problem?"

I tried to explain that this trip was a big chapter in Art's life, that he was nervous to begin with and any abrupt changes of plan were unnerving. As I spoke, I could see that Jean-Louis was obviously in an awkward spot; either he had stronger feelings for Laurence than he let on, or he had made some extraordinary promises that he was not going to be able to keep.

"So how much did she pay for the painting?"

"That's none of your business."

"Come on."

"6,000 Dollars."

"Whew. Okay, I'll work on Art. I can't promise anything and in the meantime you two should stay in a hotel."

Laurence was an extremely nice girl caught in a silly web of wills. She was fond of Jean-Louis and just wanted to be with him. After a whirlwind romance in Paris, it seemed natural for her to accompany him on our voyage. The French, without question, are the most prolific offshore sailors in the world. It is not uncommon for a French family to take a year or two on a sailing sabbatical, and an Atlantic crossing is not considered an epic achievement. Besides, the French are famous for filling every berth on a boat. If a boat sleeps eight, then they sail with a crew of eight. Poor Laurence could not understand why Art was even remotely concerned about her signing aboard.

I am, when I apply myself, very persuasive; yet I couldn't budge Art. In fact, I found myself siding with him. After all, this was his boat, his voyage, his life. The only reason he relented in allowing Jean-Louis to join us in the first place was because he was my friend. He wanted to savor the crossing and now this episode, silly as it was, was leaving a terrible taste in his mouth. I told Jean-Louis that Laurence would not be able to join us. Jean-Louis was disgusted and the two of them disappeared for a couple of days.

Molly, Art and I went about our business, topping off tanks and provisions. Fortunately, Horta is one of my favorite landfalls; the small city embracing the harbor has subtle charms that helped defuse the building stress. There is something about a tiny island port, with its manageable domain, that is perfect for landfall after a week or two of watery isolation. Continental landfalls, complete with noises, fumes and bustle are too abrupt, too bewildering. Small islands are easily appropriated, at least for a while, and I have always thought of Faial as my own.

From the yachties' paintings decorating the marina's cement walls, to narrow cobbled streets, to quaint sidewalk cafés serving strong coffee and local wines, to seas of hydrangeas bordered by neat stone walls, Faial knows how to welcome a sailor ashore. We made our way to Café Sport, the world famous watering hole where I am probably too well known. It's called Peter's locally, and we tried to drown our sorrows with a bottle of *vinho verde*, green wine, that is served very young and doesn't taste very good.

"I'll pack my bags and fly home," Art began. "I don't have anything against Laurence personally, I just don't want five people on the boat. And besides . . ."

"Art," I interrupted, "you are not going anywhere. I explained the situation to them and we'll just have to see what Jean-Louis does. If he can't come with us then so be it, but I'm sick of talking about it."

The next morning I awoke to the sound of Jean-Louis tossing his duffel bag on deck. He greeted me with a sad smile.

"I'm sorry Jean-Louis, I know you really care for her."

"Oh, Kretschmer, yes, I care for her. She is a very nice girl, but I'm sad because this cost me a lot of money."

I looked confused.

"You see, she thinks I am a very successful painter and that I'm rich or something. Anyway, I paid for her to fly back to Paris and told her that I'd fly her to Fort Lauderdale when we arrive, and with the hotel here and the dinners in Paris . . . I don't want to think about it anymore. It's time to get to sea."

The verdant peaks of Faial looked like the undulating spine of a sea serpent as we sped away from Horta under full main and 135 percent genoa. It was June 23, we were the 650th boat to call at Horta in 1987, and the only one headed west to Bermuda. While that seemed the perfect metaphor for my life, it didn't bode well for an easy passage. Twelve hours out of Horta, we were down to an 80 percent headsail and a smidgen of a main, beating into a hard southwest wind. EXCALIBUR maintained six knots but we really paid for it, pounding hard in a rising chop. The miserable motion was exhausting as the boat shuddered with each passing wave.

The southwest wind was steady at 25 to 30 knots with frequent gale-force gusts. Jean-Louis was seasick, and irritable. He had decided to use the 1800-mile passage to Bermuda to quit smoking, and now that he was trapped in a violent, smoke-free world, he was miserable. When I relieved him for the 2300 watch, he commented, "You know, Kretschmer, Laurence is a very smart girl." On our third day out of Horta, the southwest wind veered to the northeast and piped up to gale force. Although the sea was thoroughly confused, at least we were able to run before the spitting nor'easter.

The winds settled in at 40 knots true and the seas, unaccustomed to looking west, became quite agitated and rose to heights out of proportion to the wind. EXCALIBUR rolled viciously as we shot down the face of each steep wave like a giant slalom skier. Driving rain reduced visibility to a few feet beyond the eerie red and green loom on the bow. We were hand steering and each hour at the helm seemed endless. My watch was drawing to a close and I was dreaming of my warm, dry berth in the V-berth when I heard a racket astern. The spare diesels cans, which I had lashed to the stern pulpit, had wriggled loose and were crashing about.

I shouted for Jean-Louis, who had the next watch, to come

take the wheel. Soon Art and Molly were in the cockpit as well. Unfortunately, one of the five-gallon plastic cans had sprung a leak and the aft deck was covered with a sickly, stinky, slippery brew. Reaching for one can, I lost my footing and careened, fanny first, into the lifelines. I could have easily gone overboard and I was not wearing a harness. I felt a strong grip on my shoulder and before I knew it, I was being hauled back into the cockpit. This was no small feat because I displace at least 200 pounds. Jean-Louis was furious.

"Kretschmer, put your fucking harness on."

I smiled back at him, "Okay, Dulaar, anything you say. Wow, I thought you were just a wimpy artist, I never knew you were that strong."

I eventually corralled and relashed all the cans except for the leaky one which I hurled into the black night. The deck was a disaster and so was I; it was as though I had bathed in diesel fuel.

On the fifth day out of Horta, the Atlantic began to behave and soon we were sailing close-hauled across a peaceful, shimmering sea. Shipboard routines resumed. Molly scrubbed the boat with a vengeance, eliminating any trace of diesel odor. I navigated, Art talked, and Jean-Louis longed for a cigarette.

"It's not the nicotine," Jean-Louis insisted, as he ran the jib sheet through his fingers, cradling it like a cigarette. "I'm not addicted to anything. It's just that I miss smoking; that's all. It is part of my life. Only you Americans ever quit smoking; it's stupid. You think you will live forever."

I was sorry for my friend, he was having a hard time and I wished I'd had the foresight to stash a few packs of cigarettes aboard before leaving Horta. Jean-Louis and Art, however, were getting along better than I had even hoped, except for one issue, the Scotch. Jean-Louis also liked his Scotch, but all we could find in Horta was a huge jug of some foul-smelling stuff called *Abbots Choice*. Each night, while Art sipped his nectar of the gods, Jean-Louis slugged down his cheap Scotch and silently steamed.

After a week at sea, Jean-Louis was still craving a smoke and starting to drive us all crazy. I spied a ship on the horizon, it was obvious we would cross tracks fairly close and I slipped below to the chart desk. Quietly, I turned on the VHF radio and contacted the ship on Channel 16. It was a Japanese tanker, bound for the

Mediterranean. The radio officer laughed when I told him my problem.

"Hai, Hai, I understand, no problem. Let me talk captain."

When the radio officer returned he told me that as we neared each other, they would make the drop off the stern. I thanked him and returned to the cockpit.

I carefully watched the ship with the binoculars and when we were about a half mile apart, I saw a package launched from the towering stern deck.

"Hey, that ship just threw something overboard, let's tack over there and see what it is."

Art and Jean-Louis thought this was the worst idea they had ever heard, a complete waste of time.

"Kretschmer, it will take 10 minutes to come about and sail over there. For what: to look in their garbage. Are you crazy? Come on, that is 10 more minutes without a cigarette. I want to sail to Bermuda as fast as possible."

I had to invoke my captain's credentials to get them to bring the boat through the wind. Jean-Louis fished the black plastic bag out of the water with the boat hook and disgustingly pitched it on deck.

"Open it," I insisted.

With a distinct lack of enthusiasm he ripped open the bag and six cartons, 120 packs, of Marlboros fell to the deck. His eyes looked like they would pop out of his head and he erupted into delirious laughter. After I told him how I had arranged things, he kept saying, "I love the Japanese, yes, I have always loved the Japanese."

EXCALIBUR was charging across the Atlantic, but she was also drinking more of it than we liked. Her shallow bilge filled every few hours and required near constant pumping. Art and I checked all the usual leak suspects: the propeller and rudder stuffing boxes, and the through-hull fittings. We looked for signs of back pressure and tested the anti-siphon valves. Unhappily, we concluded that the centerboard trunk, or even the keelbolts themselves must be leaking. The hard pounding had caused something to work loose, a disturbing thought 800 miles from the nearest landfall. I dove over the side to look for signs of damage. While I would starve if I had to make my living as a conch diver, I did stay down long enough to report that there was no obvious problem.

Jean-Louis took over the cooking duties our second week at sea. At first, Molly was offended. But after Jean-Louis prepared fresh-caught mahi mahi, marinated in basil and garlic and served in a puffed pastry, she conceded that boat food would never be the same. Jean-Louis was a tenacious fisherman and the whine of the fishing reel became a familiar afternoon interruption. While Art appreciated the good food, the highlight of each day was his little sip of *Famous Grouse* just before sunset. One calm twilight, I lingered in the cockpit during the beginning of Jean-Louis' watch. He had prepared a marvelous fish soup for dinner and was sitting on deck, thoroughly enjoying a Marlboro.

"What is so great about the goose?" Jean-Louis asked.

"The what?"

"The goose, Art's Scotch."

"It's grouse, *Famous Grouse* and I don't know. I don't drink much Scotch."

"Well, tonight, we find out, tonight we get the goose."

"Dulaar."

"Oh come on, Kretschmer, the old man is asleep. He'll never know if we have one little glass, just one. I want to know what is so special about the goose, you know the nectar of the gods."

"Dulaar."

The devious smile and laughing blue eyes were impossible to resist.

"Okay, one little taste, but if he finds out . . ."

Jean-Louis broke out the *Famous Grouse* and poured us each a small glass. It was good. It was smooth. It did, as Art also often said, warm the cockles of your heart. And, when compared to *Abbots Choice*, it did taste like the nectar of the gods. He poured us a second small glass.

"That's it now, no more. He probably monitors the level in the bottle."

"Do you think he can tell the difference?"

"Dulaar, don't even think about it."

"Oh, come on, it will be so much fun."

It must have been the unfamiliar Scotch running around in my brain because the next thing I knew I had agreed to one more small glass, which wasn't very small, and to allow Dulaar to refill the goose bottle with *Abbots Choice*. Dulaar was giddy as he topped off the bottle and returned it to the liquor cabinet.

The next night we could barely control ourselves as Art poured out the goose, blended with mostly *Abbots Choice*. He sniffed, raised his chalice and toasted the crew. A smile cracked his lips as he took a sip. "Oh no, he knows," I was horrified.

"That is good," he declared. "It's the nectar of the gods."

On the 13th day, Bermuda decorated the horizon. We slipped through the rocky pass into lovely St. George's Harbour on July 6. In Bermuda we made some crew changes. Art convinced Mary to fly out and join us for the final 1,000-mile dash to Fort Lauderdale. Molly had had enough sailing for one summer and flew home. I dove on the keel again and this time noticed that the leading edge, where it joined the hull, had actually dropped slightly. We considered hauling EXCALIBUR in Bermuda but dreaded the delay. The forecast was for light air all the way to the coast. There was, however, a tropical depression brewing in the faraway tropics and this news hastened our departure. We were determined to beat any hurricanes to Florida. I quickly slopped a batch of underwater epoxy around the forward edge of the keel and we cleared customs. Our stay in Bermuda was just long enough to make sure Jean-Louis had plenty of cigarettes and Scotch and to fill every container we could find with diesel fuel.

Art's spirits soared with Mary aboard. Unfortunately, he insisted that she take over the galley work. Dulaar passed the apron and our fate was sealed. Mary was a wonderful woman, spry, cheerful and a fine sailor. But she wasn't much of a cook. Her specialty was hot dogs and beans, which we ate almost every day. Dulaar was in agony. I was amused. Art had only mildly complimented Jean-Louis on his culinary masterpieces, but every time Mary handed up another bowl of beans, his praise knew no bounds. While Art exclaimed to his lovely wife that each bowl of beans was better than the last, Jean-Louis rolled his eyes and muttered under his breath. There was little wind as we rumbled toward Fort Lauderdale at 2,000 RPMs, eating beans and pumping the bilge.

Two days from Fort Lauderdale, I raised Molly on the single sideband radio. I knew immediately that something was wrong from the tone of her voice.

Enjoying another gourmet meal offshore.

"John, I have bad news," she said quietly. "Real bad news."

"What is it, what's wrong?" My mind raced with horrible possibilities.

"Tim is dead."

"Tim?" I was blank for moment.

"Tim, your mom's Tim."

"Tim! Oh my god, Tim!"

The last 300 miles disappeared in a blur. I ached for my
mother. Their relationship, which at first had seemed so unlikely
to a selfish, impossible-to-please son, had grown and blossomed
during the course of their voyage. EPOCH was in Majorca, just a
tradewind passage away from completing her circumnavigation,
and now Tim, her captain and champion, was dead, and so was
their dream. He was in California, a rare trip home to visit his family. My mom was in Michigan, also visiting family. In a few days
they would rendezvous in New York and return to EPOCH. An
aneurysm exploded in his head and changed their plans forever.
There was no warning, nothing anyone could have done. It was as
sudden as if he had been shot.

My watches melted into one another as I recalled Sri Lanka,
India, Oman and, of course, the madness in Aden. I remembered
my anger, my frustration, my harsh words, and I regretted that I
didn't say the kind things that I wanted to say to him. Why does
death bring such clarity, such brutal, honest clarity? Tracking over
the long, low, summer swells, I finally understood that Tim had
loved my mother as much as I did.

*   *   *

I struggled to tie in a reef as an unlikely northwest breeze
forced SIREN'S SONG to beat north toward Grand Turk. I had
spent hours explaining to Lesa what a lovely passage it is to sail
from the Caribbean Islands back to Florida. Now here we were,
plunging into steep seas, kicking up sheets of spray. Irwin 52s
have some attributes but windward sailing is not one of them. It
was tough going and I thought Lesa was going to let me off the
hook for a while, maybe for good. I was exhausting my supply of
sea stories.

"So we are still a long way from the present. What happened
after you got back to Fort Lauderdale?" she asked and snuggled
under the dodger.

I broke out the last of the fresh cashews and a bag of pretzels for lunch.

"I moped around for a while, then drummed up another delivery. But this time it was a long one, all the way to Japan."

"Wow, but before you launch into that one, I have two questions."

"Fire away."

"Did you and Tim ever make your peace?"

"Not really, I was always going to write him a letter, but I never did. And . . ."

"And what?"

"The next question."

"And . . . did you really drink the goose?"

"Yep."

CHAPTER 6

Red Sky
by Morn

And all the while, rolling, plunging, climbing the moving
mountains and falling and wallowing in the foaming valleys,
the schooner GHOST was fighting her way farther and farther
into the heart of the Pacific—and I was on her.

JACK LONDON, The Sea-Wolf

IMET TAIJI IN THE DUSKY BAR of the Sheraton Yankee Clipper
on Fort Lauderdale Beach. In his mid-sixties, he was a jovial
Japanese man, with an easy smile and lively, dancing eyes. I
liked him immediately. His English was a lot like my Spanish: he
sounded as though he knew more than he did and our conversation was at once animated and confusing. The more excited he became, the more comically he mixed up his words. As we stumbled
out of the bar and into the tropical daylight, squinting, laughing,
shaking hands and nodding our heads, Taiji pushed an envelope
into my pocket. We were buoyant because I had just agreed to deliver his recently purchased Gulfstar 50 ketch halfway around the
world, from Fort Lauderdale to his home port near Osaka. I
walked with him to his rental car; he gave my hand, arm and entire
right side one more vigorous shaking, and said, "Captain, me you
see, Japan in."

Sitting in my car, I hastily pulled out the envelope. Delivering
a boat from Fort Lauderdale to Japan is a serious and expensive
proposition. I figured the 12,000-mile voyage would take three to
four months and I wanted to be well paid for my troubles. I had
quoted Joe, Taiji's broker, and my dear friend and tireless delivery
frontman, 15,000 Dollars all in, meaning I would cover my own

expenses unless there were problems beyond my control. I assumed the envelope contained an advance for the trip, possibly half, but likely less, and that the rest of the money would be funneled through Joe's office. I had no problem with that arrangement; I trusted Joe explicitly. To my complete surprise, I counted out 150 crisp 100-dollar bills, wrapped in a handwritten note that said, "Money extra Japan in, nice please trip. Luck good, Captain me you see, Japan in."

Fort Lauderdale seemed hotter than usual that summer and Tim's death hung over me like the dark, towering cumulus clouds that build all morning long and roll in from the Everglades with a bang every afternoon. I promised Mom that I would go to Majorca and bring EPOCH home as soon as I could, but she was in no rush, uncertain of her future plans. She had taken Tim's ashes back to the boat and cast them into the Mediterranean Sea, but that symbolic gesture had not yet eased the very real ache in her heart. When Joe called in early September and asked me if I was interested in delivering a boat to Japan, it was like a clear, cold northwest breeze pushing the summer thunderstorms out to sea. I was interested.

In what was becoming a distressing pattern, Molly was not interested in charging across the Pacific for profit. She was tired of ocean passages and did not relish the thought of sailing from Panama to Japan with a single, brief stop in Hawaii. Unfortunately, the economics of the delivery business work best for a couple; it is difficult to make money if you have to pay crew, especially on long trips. Over the years, I have cultivated a stable of friends and acquaintances who volunteer their services for the chance to obtain bluewater experience and/or be miserably seasick for a while. It is a system that works well on short deliveries; however, it is much harder to find people who can spontaneously disappear from their world for three or four months at a stretch.

There was no denying that Molly and I were struggling as a couple. We were being pulled in different directions. After every passage, she longed to settle down while I counted the days, minutes and seconds until it was time to cast off again. She was a fine sailor but the magic was missing. She felt that she had done her sea time and had a strange sense of foreboding that every new trip just might be her last. On a recent short passage up the coast, she had scribbled in the margin of my personal journal after a nasty watch,

"Tonight, I am going to fantasize about a farm and a dog and there is nothing you can do about it." Molly's dilemma was that she was fascinated by the far-flung places that were the result of our distant voyages and, like me, clung to the unlikely hope that we would somehow work things out. Guilefully exploiting her weakness, I conned her into signing on by promising that, after the passage, we would thoroughly explore Japan by land. She also extracted a promise from me that we would make a few more landfalls in the Pacific, especially between Hawaii and Japan.

I knew a third crew member was vital, at least for the first leg of the long Pacific crossing, the nearly 5,000-mile haul from Panama to Hawaii. This person had to be someone who would be able to get along in the close confines of a small boat and be both physically and psychologically ready for a 30-plus-day passage. Ideally, this person would have a great sense of humor, require little sleep, cook in any conditions and, most importantly, pay his or her own way. Then I thought of my mother, of course. Mom, the consummate woman of action and quick decisions, was uncharacteristically treading water, contemplating her next moves and quietly coming to terms with Tim's death. It didn't take much coaxing before Mom agreed to ship aboard. She would meet us in Panama and lend a hand on the long haul to Hawaii.

At first glance, the logistics of a Japanese buying an American yacht and having it delivered on its bottom all the way to Japan seemed less than efficient. However, there were several motivating factors at play. First, the cost of shipping the boat was exorbitant and significantly increased the already high import duties. Considering this, I wondered why Taiji would come all the way to America to buy a boat. True the yen was quite strong against the dollar in 1987, but it was also strong against the currencies of Taiwan, China, Australia, New Zealand, Hong Kong and other countries where sailboats were readily available and much closer to Japan. However, for some strange reason, it was fashionable in Japan's closed economy to have anything made in America. From Corvettes to American-built sailboats, Japan's new rich flaunted their Yankee products like geishas. But why a Gulfstar 50? It was a nice boat but by no means a splashy, ostentatious yacht. Taiji had recently purchased a small yacht club in Uno Ko, near Okayama City on Japan's Inland Sea. If you own a yacht club, you need a yacht, and at the time, the biggest sailboat on the Inland Sea was a 49-footer. Those were the reasons for the Gulfstar 50.

Taiji loved the boat's name and hailing port, COUNTRY GIRL, from Sioux City, Iowa. This was just the kind of Middle American kitsch sure to create a splash on the Inland Sea. Ironically, it was necessary for Taiji to officially register the boat before the delivery, so COUNTRY GIRL, with Sioux City, Iowa, plastered in gold leaf across her transom, flew the Japanese flag.

Typical of most long deliveries, the repairs dictated by the survey took longer than planned. It is a strange feeling to back a boat out of its slip for the first time, knowing that, if things go the way you hope, you won't stop again for at least eight days. By the time Molly and I pushed away from the dock on October 9, we were already a few weeks behind schedule. Once again, there would be no sea trial, no opportunity to see what worked and what didn't, and I tried not to think about the 13 through-hull fittings below the waterline. The 1,200-mile passage to Panama would serve as the sea trial.

Things did not go the way I hoped and the weather deteriorated as we approached the lower Keys. A tropical depression that was forecast to dissipate over Mexico turned right instead and was upgraded into a tropical storm. I have never accepted male names for tropical storms and Floyd, the name of a hated high school math teacher, seemed particularly offensive. Imagine having your boat or home destroyed by a storm named Floyd! If storms are going to be named after men, they should at least have names like Buster or Rocky. Unfortunately, Floyd was flexing his muscles and was on a collision course with COUNTRY GIRL, both headed for the Yucatán Channel between Mexico and Cuba. As if to spite my sexist ways, Floyd seemed intent on attaining hurricane status. I had no desire to ride out a hurricane on our second day aboard. So we ducked into Oceanside Marina on Stock Island, just east of Key West.

After we secured the last dock line, COUNTRY GIRL looked like a fly trapped in a spider's web. But our preparations were not in vain. Floyd, now a full-fledged, category-two hurricane, altered course at the last moment, passing directly over Key West and then, minutes later, Stock Island. We were blasted by steady 60- to 70-knot southwest winds and occasionally frightening gusts near 100 knots. Floyd was turning rapidly to the northeast and suddenly the

The view from the spreaders aboard COUNTRY GIRL.

wind dropped and then vanished altogether. The sun winked above. We were in the eye of the storm. Warily other crews emerged from their boats. In true Key West style, we passed around a few bottles of wine as the eerie calm lasted for about an hour. We heard the groaning wind before we felt it and scurried back to our boats to ride out the wrath of Floyd's backside.

COUNTRY GIRL survived her tempestuous encounter without even chafing a line and we departed the following day. The sea was littered with debris left in Floyd's wake but the sky was a brilliant blue, a blue that you only find in Florida after a hurricane has passed through and ripped a clean swath through the atmosphere. We were delighted as COUNTRY GIRL romped along at eight knots. Once again, I admired the versatility of the ketch rig. When the wind piped up, we usually dropped the main instead of reefing it, and maintained good speed under jib and jigger. We skirted the tip of Cuba before bearing south-southeast for Panama.

In what was the beginning of a rash of mechanical problems that would plague the entire voyage, the refrigeration system called it quits south of Cuba. While I view refrigeration as a luxury, not a necessity, I'd optimistically stocked up on frozen meat. I took the compressor and the evaporator down to bits only to realize, upon reassembly, that there were several extra, unnecessary parts. By day's end, I still could not coerce the damned thing back to life so we began to eat like condemned criminals: ham and sausage for breakfast, chicken and ribs for lunch, and steak and pork chops for dinner. The toughest decision of the passage was choosing what to eat and what to feed to the fish.

Molly spotted the massive breakwalls off the Canal Zone at first light on October 21, which would prove to be a fateful day. As we eased COUNTRY GIRL stern-to at the rickety Panama Canal Yacht Club dock, we learned that a nationwide strike was just underway. The people of Panama were trying to force the ouster of their dictator *du jour*, General Manuel Noriega. They naively and completely underestimated his resolve and the word was out in the Canal Zone that the pock-faced *generalissimo* was going to violently crush the demonstrations later in the day. The atmosphere around the yacht club was tense as the U. S. authorities had issued a "Code Charlie—Personnel Movement Restriction," meaning that all Americans in Panama were to stay in Cristobal, the Zone, and were not to be seen in public. While it was typical of me to stumble into a country just in time for a coup d'état, what made the situation even more intriguing was that my mother's plane was set to arrive at noon.

The airport was in Panama City, 45 miles away across the Isthmus. Mom was already in the air by the time we cleared customs and I had no chance to call home. She would be arriving in a couple of hours and I was desperate to find a ride to Panama City. No taxi drivers would even consider taking me to the airport and I was told that I would probably be arrested if I attempted to take the train. *La Guardia*, the police, were firmly under the imposing thumb of the *generalissimo*, who, with a complete lack of originality, was trying to blame Panama's dreadful economic conditions on the United States. Although the general populace wasn't buying his propaganda, the police were and an especially nasty group of cops, nicknamed 'the Dobermen', were his henchmen.

Doing what I always do when I'm desperate, I retreated to the bar. Webster's could put "Panama Canal Yacht Club" after the word seedy and have the perfect definition; naturally I liked the place. The bar was packed with nervous gringos. I cut my way through the smoke and took a seat at the bar. The Chinaman was working behind the bar. The Chinaman, as everyone called him, had been cooking at the club for as long as anyone could remember. He winked at me knowingly for I'd been through the canal five times before. I've never seen the Chinaman without a cigarette and an ash equally as long dangling from his mouth. It's best not to think about how often the ashes end up in the chop suey.

A clean cut young man, obviously in the military, sat down next to me. Bruce told me that he worked for "a part of the Department of Defense that you don't want to know about." Of course, the mere fact that he told me this made me highly suspect of him, but he did seem well informed about the crisis and I was hungry for news. "It's all quiet in the city, but I doubt it will last. The Dobermen will create a demonstration if they have to, just so they'll have somebody to kill."

When I told him about my mother's imminent arrival, he just shook his head.

"I've got to get to Panama City," I said. "I mean it's my mother, she's 66 years old, for God's sake."

"I wouldn't take a chance out on the streets, not today."

"I've got to take a chance. Is it really that bad out there?"

Bruce then proceeded to tell me in great detail several horror stories of how the Dobermen had tortured anti-Noriega *politicos*. I finally interrupted.

"I don't give a damn about the local politics. I just want to be sure my mother is safe," adding after glancing at my watch, "and she lands in an hour."

"You might be able to bribe a taxi driver and ride in the trunk. Or better yet, if we can reach your mother at the airport, it would be safer if she rode over here in the trunk because it will be easier getting out of the city. It's probably impossible to get in."

"In the trunk? My mother?"

He just shrugged his shoulders before mumbling, "And it'll be expensive, maybe 500 Dollars, and just pray to God there is not a roadblock."

The pothole was invented in Panama and the road between Colón and Panama City is tough enough to survive in the front seat. The thought of my mother riding in the trunk was beyond comprehension. I resolved to make my way to the train station and take my chances with the Dobermen. After fortifying myself with a stiff gin and tonic, I thanked Bruce for his time and pushed off my bar stool. Just then the doors to the bar swung open and in walked my mom, flanked by two uniformed policemen.

"Johnny," she sang out, smiling, "it's great to see you." After we hugged, she introduced me to her friends. "I was able to catch an earlier flight out of Miami and these nice young men gave me a ride from the airport." It seems the policemen were on their way to Colón and concerned about her riding in a taxi so they gave her a personal escort. I was bewildered; my mother's cheer can conquer the world. The policemen obviously felt out of place. I thanked them and shook their hands before they quickly slipped out the back door. Back at the bar, Bruce was nowhere to be seen.

General Noriega succeeded, the proposed nationwide strike never took root and although there were scattered demonstrations in the city that night, when the tropical sun rose the next morning, he was still the big *jefe* and the Canal Zone was back in operation. I made my way to the offices of the Panama Canal Commission and began the tedious official process of preparing for the transit. Unfortunately, COUNTRY GIRL had not been through the canal previously and thus required an admeasurement. This arcane system of measurement apparently has some usefulness in assessing the cargo-carrying capacity of a ship. On a yacht, however, it is silly protocol for the extraction of money. Once admeasured, you pay your fees, which in those days were still quite cheap, less than 200 Dollars, and schedule a transit.

Canal rules require four 100-foot dock lines, stout cleats, adequate fendering and four line-handlers in addition to the helmsman. We enlisted the help of Felix and Vincent. Felix was Venezuelan, singlehanding an old Morgan 27 Quarter Tonner, bound for New Zealand and full of life. He told dramatic stories in terrible English, arms flailing about for effect, and flirted shamelessly with Molly. Vincent, a serious young man from Brittany, had emigrated to Calgary in western Canada and had spent seven years building a steel boat. He then trucked it 800 miles to the nearest saltwater and was on his way to Florida. His personality was as dull and dependable as his boat. They were excellent line handlers and good enough company.

Although it is only 45 miles between oceans, the Panama Canal Authority decided that they could employ two pilots if they turned the transit into a two-day affair. Our first pilot, who was two hours late, introduced himself and then said he didn't want to know our names because he hoped he would never see us again. He was disgusted that he was relegated to piloting 'toys' through the canal. We were fortunate to raft alongside a tug for the ride up through the first three lock chambers. About 100 feet above the level of the nearby Caribbean, we anchored in Gatun Lake for the night. It was a treat to swim in fresh water, even if I did nearly kill myself. With both national and captain's pride at stake, and trying not let Felix outdo me, I dove off a platform that had to be 75 feet above the water. My entry was not graceful and my head felt like I'd gone 15 rounds with Mike Tyson. The next morning, a cheerful young tugboat captain, in training to become a pilot, arrived right on time and we completed our canal transit. In a driving torrent, we dropped Felix and Vincent at the Balboa Yacht Club and continued into the Pacific. Our next landfall, Hilo, on the big island of Hawaii, was just out of sight, 4,500 miles away.

The Central American coastline was dreary. Prolonged calms interrupted by nasty squalls forced us to burn precious fuel motoring day after day. I was thankful that we had radar, as visibility was often reduced to a few hundred feet. But we could still monitor the ships pouring in and out of the separation scheme leading to the canal. We carried the signature of most boats that transit the canal: yellow plastic, two-gallon cooking oil containers turned into spare fuel cans. We had 20 sprinkled about the aft deck. A couple days out, the Benmar autopilot started steering back toward Panama. It was an ancient, photo voltaic unit with a burned-out bulb and no hope of repair. I rigged up the belt-driven Autohelm 3000, which is a vital part of my delivery kit, and wondered how it would steer a 35,000-pound boat when we picked up the trades.

We searched for the heralded northeast trades in every zephyr and flew the spinnaker at every opportunity. Whenever the wind blew for more than hour, I confidently announced that we were in the trades. Invariably, an hour later we were under power again. Even when motoring, our progress was unreliable as the Perkins diesel had developed an annoying air leak and I never knew when it would sputter to a stop. It didn't really matter. After 11 days we still had 3,000 miles to go and a total of 35 gallons of fuel remaining, just enough for the generator to charge the batteries.

Finally, on November 15, about halfway to Hilo, the trades emerged with a vengeance. COUNTRY GIRL sprang to life. With the 120 percent genoa poled out and the mizzen trimmed to help the Autohelm cope, we ripped off 1,700 miles in 10 days. The winds were steady between 25 and 35 knots and the seas raged. I am not one to overestimate wave heights, but the majestic combers marauding across the North Pacific were at least 20 and often 30 feet. The ride was rugged, as COUNTRY GIRL rolled from gunwale to gut-wrenching gunwale. We had several bizarre visitors hitch a ride, including a wayward heron and an exhausted osprey.

Mom and Molly both put a lot of stock in the color of sunrise and sunset, and night after night the sun would disappear into the gray banks of clouds lining the western sky without a trace of red, only to reappear 12 hours later bathed in horizon-sweeping magenta. This was not a good way to begin another day of cavorting on our oceanic giant slalom course, and they would try to convince themselves that the sky was not really as red as it looked. My mood was determined more by progress than sky color and despite the miserable living conditions, COUNTRY GIRL was consistently logging 165 to 175 miles a day. I was content. But our wild roller-coaster ride came to an abrupt halt on the morning of November 24, 27 days at sea and still 750 miles from Hilo.

The wind was gusting to gale force and I was giving the Autohelm the morning off. Surfing down the face of a huge wave, COUNTRY GIRL pegged at 10 knots on the speedo. I steered hard to port to bring us back on course, but COUNTRY GIRL would not respond. I steered to starboard, nothing. There was no steering! Out of control, COUNTRY GIRL flirted with broaching before rounding up into the wind with the sails flogging madly. As I dashed below, I considered the possibilities: The steering cables might have slipped a sheave, or parted; or, God forbid, we had damaged the rudder. I flung open the engine room doors to look at the bottom of the pedestal. There was the steering chain lying on the diesel, in two pieces. One of the links had broken. This was a problem I hadn't considered, but a cable steering system without a pedestal chain is about as useful as a bicycle without the sprocket chain. Short of damaging the rudder, this was the worst possible scenario.

The rudder was crashing back and forth and Molly and I hurried to the aft cabin to affix the emergency tiller. I carefully moved the six-foot brass dolphin that Taiji had insisted on buying in Lauderdale and which shared the aft bunk with us, and then recklessly tore off the bedding and bolted the tiller in place. What a joke. Try steering a 35,000-pound boat in 20-foot following seas with a three-foot-long tiller—from the aft cabin! I told Molly to hold the tiller for a second while I dashed up on deck to take the spare compass below. But before I got out of the aft cabin, she was flung into the hanging locker. It was impossible for her to hold the tiller and even together, it was nearly impossible to steer. We careened from side to side as Mom shouted directions from the cockpit, "Port, no, back to starboard, no, more to port."

Finally, we managed to lash the tiller to the mizzen mast and with only a reefed mizzen set, coaxed the boat into a hove-to position. The emergency tiller was useless. If we were going to get to Hawaii, I had to repair the pedestal steering system. Of course, we did not have a spare chain, or a master link, so I scoured the spare

parts and found a small sail shackle that, with the help of a hammer, might be persuaded to become a chain link. After bending the
shackle into shape, I began reassembling the steering system, which
was tough going as COUNTRY GIRL bucked about in towering seas.
I was working flat on my back and sprawled across the diesel. After
several hours of dropping tools and cursing, I had the system back
together.

I removed the emergency tiller and shouted for Molly to take
the helm. Something was wrong, she was steering like a drunk, frantically turning the wheel and unable to hold a course. When she
steered right, COUNTRY GIRL went left and vice versa. No! I had
connected the wrong cable ends to the chain. At that moment I
longed for my soft yacht broker days. The thought of disconnecting
the entire system inspired us to try to steer in reverse; hell, it was
only 750 miles to Hilo. Although we tried to think of the wheel as
a tiller, it just didn't work. After a few hours, we were exhausted and
cutting an ever-widening S-path through the Pacific. At that rate we
would double the distance to Hilo and go crazy from trying to think
backwards. Thoroughly disgusted, we heaved-to again. Mom
cooked up a colossal batch of spaghetti, we polished off two bottles
of red wine and, throwing caution to the tradewinds, slept through
the night without a watch. I tackled the repair in the morning and
before noon we were underway.

No sooner did we begin charging toward Hawaii than the last
autopilot belt snapped. Mom spent hours ingeniously mending it,
but with the winds still steady at 30 knots, it never lasted long.
Molly and I hand steered the last five days, which seemed more like
five years, before the towering summits of Mauna Loa and Kea
greeted us just before sunset (which of course was not red) on our
33rd day at sea. I managed to start the diesel in the morning and,
dreaming of hot showers and cold beers, we eased into Hilo's inner
yacht harbor. Just as we eased COUNTRY GIRL alongside the quay,
the dockmaster came running out of his office.

"You'll have to clear out of here," he shouted in a panicked
voice. "There's a tsunami warning."

"A what?"

"Tsunami, caused by an earthquake in Alaska. It can spawn
tidal waves down here. It's safe two miles out to sea but here in
the harbor," he closed his eyes and shook his head, "son, it can be

devastating. Believe me, I was here in '56, the water was above that building over there."

I was incredulous and confused but, after 34 days, Mom and Molly were dead set against returning to sea, not even for a few hours. "I'll take my chances in the tsunami," Molly announced brazenly before adding, "I'd rather drown in a bar than spend another 30 minutes aboard this boat." Luckily, I was spared the potentially dangerous task of coaxing them back aboard and heading back to sea when a Coast Guard cutter steamed into the harbor and announced that the warning had just been canceled.

We stayed in Hilo long enough to have a new steering chain and a dozen spare autopilot belts shipped out. We were sorry to see Mom skip ship. She had been a stalwart crew member and, even during the lowest moments of the long passage, kept our spirits up and our bellies full. The night before we were set to depart a strong offshore wind created a dangerous surge in the harbor. Several of the boats that were lying stern-to at the wall dragged anchor, including COUNTRY GIRL. Chaos reigned as boats pounded into the concrete wall and each other. I launched the dinghy and rowed our longest anchor line to an outer mooring. While my brain power is often questioned, my arm power isn't. Somehow I managed to pull COUNTRY GIRL off the wall. I collapsed into my bunk, knowing that I had pulled too hard; something didn't feel quite right. But there was no time to worry about it, I had a boat to deliver and Japan was still 4,000 miles away.

My log entry of 0900 on December 10 was cheerful: "Clear of Hilo, the sailing is pleasant, winds light but steady; the sun is even shining. We're planning a brief stop in Wake Island but I can taste Japan. Spectacular sight ahead, Madam Pele is doing her thing. The Puu Kukui volcano is still erupting and we see the lava snaking down hillside and plunging into the sea."

The next entry is not until 0400 on December 12: "Hove-to, riding out a full gale—I mean full, like Force 10-full—200 miles south of Honolulu. Last night was a terrible night. How could so many things go wrong so quickly?"

After clearing the south shore of the big island, we shaped a west-northwest course designed to skirt the entire Hawaiian archipelago, which, incidentally, has numerous isolated islets and shoals and stretches nearly 1,000 miles to Midway Island. A fierce north-

COUNTRY GIRL arrives in Hilo, on the big island of Hawaii.

west gale galloped down from the Arctic and clobbered COUNTRY GIRL. Within a span of four hours, the mizzen sheet parted and the mizzen boom nearly sheared the gooseneck fitting, the steering cables slipped a sheave, the diesel overheated and shut down, the generator starting spitting fuel like a cobra and, for a crescendo, the furling headsail exploded. We needed a reprieve and when the gale moderated, we limped into Ala Wai Yacht Basin in Honolulu. We arrived just in time for, later that day, another full gale engulfed the islands. Unfortunately, the impatient delivery skipper of a Swan 65 outbound from California decided against heaving-to and tried to run the treacherous entrance channel into the yacht harbor. Several of us made our way to the jetty and watched with horror as a powerful breaker sent the Swan skidding into the reef. I helped the Coast Guard with the rescue effort, which took all day and, luckily, nobody was seriously injured. The Swan, however, was a total loss.

Molly and I spent three therapeutic weeks in Honolulu celebrating Christmas and the New Year. We gradually put COUNTRY GIRL back together. I cabled Taiji and explained what had happened and within 24 hours, he wired money for a new sail and complete overhauls of the engine and generator. Just before we

A bunch of nuts in Hawaii.

were ready to depart, he sent an urgent message to the dockmaster. He requested that we detour to Guam, in the Marianas Islands, where he would meet us and join us for the final leg to Japan. Sailing to Guam added 1,500 miles to the voyage and changed the dynamics of the next leg. Guam straddles the 13th parallel. By steering south-southwest from Hawaii, it was likely that we would pick up kinder and gentler tradewinds and have warm weather. By straying back into the heart of the tropics however, there was a reasonable chance that we'd encounter a typhoon. Still, it wasn't difficult to talk Molly out of abandoning our plans to call at Wake Island. I had been planning a more direct, and, no doubt, colder route to Japan. She packed away the woolies and we headed straight for Guam, a mere 3,400 miles distant, which we hoped to spy in about 25 days.

The passage to Guam was the antithesis of the boisterous run to Hawaii. At last Neptune shed pity on the crew of COUNTRY GIRL. We blasted out of Honolulu and averaged 150 miles a day before crossing the International Dateline on January 12. This was tradewind sailing at its best. The night watches slipped by under a dome of stars. Curious and truly pelagic birds hailing from Micronesian islands, which were just close enough to our track to be in their range, paid us daily visits. Before we reached the Eastern Hemisphere, I read 12 books, an eclectic list ranging from *Zorba the Greek* by Nikos Kazantzakis, (which still lingers as my favorite all-time book—a big statement) to the incredibly depressing *Handmaid's Tale* by Margaret Atwood. A week after crossing the dateline, however, we had a scare that emphasized just how alone you really are at sea.

I'd been feeling listless for a few days when I began to have severe chest pains and lost feeling in the left side of my body. Lying in my berth and wedged against the big brass dolphin, I was burning with fever one minute, and the next, I was clammy cold. My symptoms were ominously strokelike. Although we had extensive medical supplies aboard, with the arrogance of youth, we didn't have even the simplest first-aid manual. Molly doubled up on watches and drove the boat as hard as she dared; she was scared. She wrote in the log, "I feel so helpless. If something happens, we're 900 miles from anyplace with a name."

Fortunately, I began to perk up as we neared Guam. And it

was just in time because the weather began to deteriorate. We picked up the BBC and learned that we were encountering the tail end of Typhoon Roy, which, only days before, had ravaged Guam with 150-mph winds. There it was again, those damned male storms causing havoc in my life: a typhoon added to an already impressive list of natural disasters encountered on one delivery. On our 23rd day at sea, we made our way into a lovely, wide harbor some distance from the main town of Agana. After clearing at the commercial quay, where the U.S. customs officers found our official Japanese registration papers amusing, we dropped the hook in front of the quaint Marianas Yacht Club. The anchor had barely hit the bottom before Taiji came charging out from shore in a borrowed dinghy wearing a smile and a 'I survived Typhoon Roy' T-shirt.

Molly was ready to abandon the delivery in Guam. Not because she was thoroughly tired of the long haul, she was; and not because she dreaded the last 1,500 miles up to Japan, she did; but because she was convinced something was seriously wrong with me. I checked into a medical clinic and a kindly Filipino doctor examined me from every angle. He couldn't find anything wrong and suggested that I was suffering from exhaustion, and had probably suffered sunstroke as well. His diagnosis seemed logical to me. I knew that in pulling COUNTRY GIRL off the wall in Hilo I had summoned every ounce of strength in my body and hadn't felt right since. Exhausted or not, I was determined to steer COUNTRY GIRL into Japanese waters. I was going to see the sun rise in the land of the rising sun.

We spent a about a week in Guam, giggling at the Japanese honeymooners decked out in cowboy gear, and wondering how long it would take before the obvious mission to pave over the entire island with duty free shops would be complete. The island was also under siege by pesky brown snakes and the customs officer suggested we carefully check the bilge to make sure we didn't have a stowaway. On February 1, 1988, we set off for Kii Suido, the strait between Shikoku and Honshu, and the eastern approach to the Inland Sea.

Taiji looked great but felt terrible. He had all the latest gear for sailing. Molly and I couldn't help but laugh when he turned up for watch clad in full Henri Lloyd foulweather gear, complete with a prototype inflatable safety harness. He had binoculars draped around his neck, two personal strobes strapped around his biceps, and a dive knife lashed to his leg. He had acupressure bracelets and a patch behind his ear in a double-whammy effort to ward off *mal de mer*. He looked like he was ready for a passage to the moon, or at least Cape Horn, although at the time we were reaching before a generous 15-knot tradewind and the temperature hovered around 80 degrees. Unfortunately, four hours later he was curled up on the main saloon settee, and there he stayed for the next seven days. Molly, who was delighted at the prospect of sharing watch duties, was thoroughly disgusted as Taiji refused to budge. He was missing the best sailing of the entire voyage. COUNTRY GIRL reeled off two 200-mile days to start the passage, but Taiji remained in the fetal position, oblivious to the water rushing under the keel.

Three days out of Guam, Taiji mysteriously remembered a business meeting that he had to attend and suggested that we detour to Okinawa, a left turn that would add still more miles to the voyage and, worse, make the final approach into the Inland Sea more of a beat. Unfortunately, I had both the chart for Naha, the main harbor, and sympathy for our useless crewman. We slacked the sheets and made our way toward Okinawa-Jima. Miraculously, as soon as we sighted the ugly plumes of smoke rising from the industrial skyline of Naha, Taiji began to feel better. With land in sight, he was bounding about the deck. By the time we secured COUNTRY GIRL to the ragged quay in the fishing harbor, he was positively beaming. Although I can never be sure, he seemed to be telling sea stories to the fishermen crowding around the boat.

Back in his natural element, Taiji was kindly to a fault and seemed to forget about his critical meeting. Anything Molly (he pronounced it Mawree) looked at, Taiji bought for her. He clearly felt guilty about his less than sterling sailing performance. But we had no desire to tarry in Okinawa, the end of our odyssey was in sight; we were ready to write the final chapter. We waved goodbye to Taiji and sailed out into the East China Sea. Unrolling a new chart, I realized that the Orient had snuck up on me: We were only 500 miles from Hong Kong, 300 miles from Taiwan, and 250 miles from Shanghai. Okinawa lies about halfway down Ryukyu Retto, a chain of islands that reaches southwest from Kyushu toward Taiwan. February 1988 was not a good time to be sailing north in the East China Sea. For some masochistic reason, I was reading Conrad's *Typhoon* at the time. The narrator tries to warn cavalier Captain MacWhirr by subtly noting, "The China seas are narrow seas. They are seas full of every-day, eloquent facts; such as islands, sand-banks, reefs, swift and changeable currents—tangled facts that nevertheless speak to a seaman in clear and definite language."

The only thing he forgot to add was that they are also seas raked by incessant winter gales. Having beat down the English Channel in December, pounded my way up the Red Sea in February, and doubled Cape Horn to windward, I was no stranger to tough going. But the icy wind and square waves that blasted us day after day in the 'narrow' East China Sea equaled the fury of any ocean I'd tasted.

Luckily, our windspeed meter topped out at 50 knots; I didn't want to know if it blew more than that. Unfortunately, our thermometer did read below 40 degrees, as temperatures were usually in the mid- to low-30s. It was best not to calculate or even think about the windchill factor. From Okinawa to Amami O Shima, to Yaku Shima, toward Tanega Shima, COUNTRY GIRL fought her way ever closer to a long rest on quiet seas. Landfall at Tanega Shima was one for the archives. After a voyage of 12,000 miles, how could three stinking, miserable miles seem so long?

We had been beating all day so we closed to within three miles of the low-slung, rocky island, hoping for some protection from the lee. The wind was blowing straight out of the harbor and, weary of tacking, we dropped all sail save the mizzen and attempted to power into port. It took two full hours of plunging and thrusting, kicking up sheets of spray, and being brought to a dead stop by samurai waves. By all rights, we should have had a lee, but some sort of oriental trick made the waves skirt the land and pile up on COUNTRY GIRL's bow. When we finally found some protection, we could not spot the harbor markers while the Sailing Directions warned against an unfamiliar approach. Just when I was considering heading back to deep water, a seemingly accommodating fishing boat steamed out of the harbor and led us to the approach channel. We lumbered into the tiny fishing harbor and rafted alongside a couple of small but stout and well-kept steel fishing boats. Our fishing boat turned out to be a service boat for the

Bundled up for the cold approach to Japan.

Japanese space program which had its launch site on Tanega Shima. They had been tracking us on radar because we had inadvertently sailed perilously close to a maximum danger zone. The paper they handed me called it a 'high impact falling debris zone' caused from a launch earlier in the day. We were nonplussed. If a piece of rocketship jetsam fell out of the sky and sank COUNTRY GIRL, after encounters with Hurricane Floyd, General Noriega, a tsunami, an erupting volcano and Typhoon Roy, then it was meant to be.

We tarried a day in peaceful Tanega Shima. The fishermen were amazed that just two of us were sailing such a large boat, and, amazingly, one of us was a woman. That couldn't be. They wanted to know if the other men were hiding below, or had they jumped overboard? Once sure that we were alone, they were gracious hosts and insisted on giving us charts, fresh food and several bottles of saki. The language of the sea has no boundaries and, although we could not understand more than a few words despite my tenacious study of a book called *Coping With Japan*, we communicated just fine. The fishermen led us to their lovely Shinto shrine on a bluff overlooking the sea. Desperate to reach Kyushu, I made a private pact with Benten, the Japanese goddess of the sea. Known as a fickle deity, she is the only female of the seven gods of good luck and can bring fair or foul winds depending on her mood.

On February 18, we set off for the tiny port of Aburatsu on the southeast coast of Kyushu and our new final destination. Because of the protracted nature of the voyage, I called Taiji from Tanega Shima and told him that Aburatsu was going to have to be the end of the road. He was disappointed but he didn't have much leverage after his feeble performance on the passage from Guam. We had non-refundable return tickets and my promise to Molly to spend time exploring Japan by land had already been whittled down to less than two weeks. We would travel by train and car from Aburatsu to Tokyo.

Greedy goddess Benten took my prayers but offered no sympathy in return and the final 50 miles of the voyage may have been the most challenging. We beat north against a fresh gale, and after a tiresome bout with the contrary Black Current, followed the well-lit coast until we spotted the harbor range lights around midnight. Molly steered the range and I was glued to the radar as we threaded our way through a narrow opening into an

Looking for advice and fair winds at a Shinto shrine on Amami-o-Shima.

expansive harbor. The night was black and there was no obvious place to tie up so we ceremoniously dropped the anchor in the middle of the harbor and cracked open a bottle of saki. It was first light before we finally polished off the bottle and a reluctant dawn crept above the horizon. By the way, there was not a hint of red in the cold, leaden sky.

*　　*　　*

The wind died as quickly as it started and I had to rebuild the fuel system before we could coax SIREN'S SONG big diesel back to life. The floorboards were ajar as I routed a fuel line from the generator to the main engine and the sweet smell of diesel fuel filled the cabin. Our luxury yacht was beginning to look, and smell, very much like a typical boat on delivery, with jury-rigged systems taking precedence over all else. We were making our way toward what is now gallantly called the Christopher Columbus Passage, a wide, deep pass between Grand Turk and South Caicos Islands, and was formerly known before the quincentennial hoopla of 1992, as the rather workmanlike Turks and Caicos Passage.

After we finally reached Japan, Lesa was silent.

"There's more, believe it or not. Do you want to hear it?"

"Sure."

"Well, the next morning, attempting to back COUNTRY GIRL stern-to a quay, I fouled both the prop and the skeg on submerged mooring lines. I had to cut one of the lines and in the process cast about 20 little fishing boats adrift. It was pandemonium in the harbor."

"Oh, God, what happened?"

"Right at that moment the customs boat pulled alongside and four guys jumped aboard. They didn't care about the fishing boats and without a word began dismantling COUNTRY GIRL. They took the leads off the fuel and water tanks and peered inside with a little scope. Then one of the officers—and they all looked identical in neat blue suits with black ties—started to drill a hole in the main bulkhead. I screamed at him but he just smiled at me and nodded. He took out another scope and probed around in the hollow area behind the bulkhead. Convinced that we were not hiding drugs or anything else on Japan's long list of illegal things to bring into their 'pure' country, he took a teak bung out of his briefcase, tapped it into the hole, and even gave it a few swipes of varnish!"

"What was happening to all the fishing boats?"

"While I was fussing with customs, somebody had contacted a chap named Yoshinaga, who arrived on the scene in a Mustang convertible. He leaped out of the car as if he was in a movie, surveyed the scene, and then dove into the freezing water. He retrieved his boat first and then used it to round up all the others. It was impressive."

"Was he furious with you?"

"No, in fact, he was so excited to meet a living, breathing Yank, he took us to his house afterwards and his wife gave me a bath and massage. Then she prepared a traditional Japanese meal. It was a nice way to wind up the voyage."

Lesa was disgusted. "I can't believe it. Do you remember our conversation about luck? I rest my case."

CHAPTER 7

She Drives Me Crazy

Our immediate reaction was to give up any further attempts to reach shelter and to decide to take our chances with the storm at sea. However, a little reflection changed our minds. HAPPY ADVENTURE was leaking so badly that the unreliable pump was barely able to hold its own. The engine was clearly on its last legs. The wind was rising out of the sou'east. We knew we would stand no chance of beating offshore into the teeth of mounting wind and seas. One way or another we seemed destined to go ashore; only the choice of how we did it remained to us.

FARLEY MOWAT, The Boat Who Wouldn't Float

"ROGER, IF YOU WANT MY ADVICE, save your money and skip the TransArc. We don't need a silly rally to sail across the Atlantic. I'm sure Jimmy Cornell is a nice guy but he's becoming the Arthur Frommer of offshore sailing. He's organizing something that shouldn't be organized. I don't like the idea of turning an ocean crossing into a If-it's-Tuesday-this-must-be-Bermuda travel tour group."

"I always want your advice, John," Roger responded in a creaky, Carolina accented voice that belied his considerable size. "But, as you know, I may not take it."

Five years before I had taught Roger and his lovely wife Myrna coastal and celestial navigation at my school in Fort Lauderdale. They had spent the ensuing years cruising the Bahamas. Now Roger was prepared to take his boat HERE AND NOW, a Henry Scheel-designed Morgan 45, to the Mediterranean and asked me to skipper it. Believe it or not, I was ready for another passage. Having returned from Japan a month and a half before, I could already feel the sweaty grip of land life closing in on me. Besides, sailing across the Atlantic struck me as the logical way to get to Spain. I promised my mother that in the fall I would bring home her boat, EPOCH, which was still lying in Majorca. Mom, who at age 67 had just joined the crew of an oceanic research ship plying the Gulf of Alaska, was in no rush to deal with the boat and told me to take my time. Never one for long-range planning, however, I did like the look of the upcoming year: an eastbound Atlantic crossing in May, a summer exploring the Med in EPOCH, a westbound crossing in November, and, if my money held out, a winter in the Caribbean. I knew that a delivery or two would turn up along the way and that I'd sell a few articles about the Japan delivery to keep food on the table. All in all, I felt rather smug at keeping the real world at bay for at least another year. Molly, however, was not ready for more sea duty and we made vague plans to rendezvous in Spain.

Roger, who is one of my favorite people, prepared for the transatlantic passage with the same thoroughness that has made him a success in business. First, he had all the gear aboard HERE AND NOW serviced. Then he made a list of every conceivable piece of equipment that he didn't already have and that we might possibly need on the crossing. He purchased everything on the list. Then, for good measure, he purchased everything again, for the spare-parts inventory. He issued each crew member a notebook— a thick notebook—detailing the location of everything aboard. HERE AND NOW, not a swift vessel to begin with, sank ever lower into the water and became a little slower with each trip to the chandlery. While I would come to question some of Roger's outfitting and equipment decisions during the month-long crossing, his choice of crew couldn't have been better. Unfortunately, my choice of mate/cook could hardly have been worse.

For each leg, Roger arranged for a different friend from his hometown of Winston-Salem, North Carolina, to join us as crew. Penn signed on for the Miami-to-Bermuda leg. A soft-spoken lawyer, Penn is an example of why that profession was once so well respected. A southern gentleman, Penn was just the right crew combination, a good sailor and good company. The mate/cook, whom I will call Gary, was, unfortunately, in over his head before we even slipped our mooring in the shoal waters fronting the Miami Yacht Club. I had sold him a boat during my brief brokering stint. It was a rugged, 36-foot cutter that he planned to sail around the world. As with many first-time boat owners, only the small detail of learning to sail stood between him and his lofty goal. Gary was a nice enough guy and anxious for bluewater experience. He jumped at my offer to crew on the passage.

"This is a working trip, not a pleasure trip," I explained, not mincing words. "Our job is to get this boat to Gibraltar, period. Your second job is to help me with whatever I'm doing, without questioning or complaining, especially during those lovely times at 0200 when all hell is breaking loose. Your first job, however, is to cook. It's really not very glamorous, Gary. Are you sure you want to do this?"

"Absolutely, John, this is the opportunity of a lifetime."

I knew I was in trouble when Gary showed up with 30 matching outfits. I had told him to plan for roughly 30 days but offshore sailing requires a high degree of flexibility. Matching outfits, right down to color-coordinated socks, is not a sign of flexibility. In Gary's defense, although he was completely unprepared for the crossing, he looked great. He had read all the cruising books and sounded like an expert, but he didn't have any experience to back up his big talk. Still, I have discovered many times over the years that sailing experience is much less important aboard a small boat than life experience. But his life experience was also limited. In his early 40s, he had worked for a huge corporation all his life, anonymously collecting his paycheck year after year and all the while preparing for his escape. His dream had been incubating for so long that by the time it was ready to hatch, he was too shackled to his yuppie gods to get up off the egg. He subscribed to all the right magazines, he could quote from back issues of *Practical Sailor*, he had all the buzzwords and, of course, he wore all the right clothes. He was smart enough to know that he needed this crossing, especially in a boat that defied most of the parameters for bluewater, as laid out in his bible, *Cruising World*. But he just didn't have the gumption or flexibility to pull it off with any style.

Roger didn't take my advice and we joined the TransArc Rally. Jimmy Cornell is intense and good at what he does, but I just don't respond well to being herded about like a sea cow. To my surprise, most of the skippers thrived on relinquishing the control and organization of their passage to Jimmy, and also anticipated chatting en route via SSB and VHF with other rally members. I am a sociable creature, especially ashore; however, at sea I relish the private nature of a passage. The last thing I want to do is talk with another skipper on the radio net about how to season chicken à la King or fret over a distant weather forecast. In an emergency, I am the first person to respond. But otherwise, I like to celebrate my own feasts or, if Gary is the cook, lack thereof, and don't need the anxiety of someone else's weather concerns poisoning my optimism.

Gary Jobson would have been impressed with my start. Miraculously, HERE AND NOW was first over the line. The TransArc Rally was underway. There were only seven boats in our fleet but the plan was to link up with another dozen boats in Bermuda that had just departed Antigua. Then, Neptune forbid, we would sail en masse across the pond. Despite favorable conditions, 30 knots off the starboard quarter, within 30 minutes, we were bringing up the rear of the fleet.

Six hours later, the winds clocked to the north as a rare late-spring cold front turned the Gulf Stream into choppy mayhem. HERE AND NOW hobbled to weather as Gary assumed a prone position on the leeside cockpit bench, the only comfortable spot on deck, and there he remained for three days. Roger, Penn and I scurried about tending to one mechanical problem after another, the most serious of which was a wayward autopilot. Just for the crossing, Roger had installed a new Robertson model but the hydraulic pump gave out on day two. We installed a backup Navico, belt-driven wheel pilot but it couldn't cope with the Morgan's hydraulic steering. Gary was unable to cope with job one, so most of the cooking duties fell to me. Roger refused to have propane on his boat and opted for an electric cooker instead. Just to heat water for coffee required firing up the generator. We did all our cooking in the microwave and, fortunately, Myrna had prepared several meals in advance. Familiar Bermuda decorated the horizon after seven and a half days. For the record, we were not the last boat to arrive; that distinction loomed ahead.

The governor general attended the TransArc party at the St. George's Dinghy Club. Ruddy faced, he was a stiff, cardboardlike character, sculpted from the pages of some stereotypical guidebook describing how to look and act like a proper colonial administrator. An incredibly boring chap, at Jimmy Cornell's prompting, he informed us in painstaking detail that we were all part of an historic event, the first sailing rally to link the historic harbors of Gibraltar, St. George's and English Harbour. Upstart and slightly indecent Miami was conveniently omitted. Jimmy Cornell then wrestled away the microphone and told ralliers several more reasons why this was an historic event. I must confess I didn't hear what they were, as I slipped out the back door, jumped on my scooter, and headed down the hill to the White Horse Tavern.

We were the fourth boat over the line for the start of leg two, a 1,800-mile passage to Horta in the lovely Azores. Rocky, who was a great shipmate and the least staid banker I'd ever met, signed on for leg two. Rocky was everything Gary was not. He tackled any problem with energy and humor, always overstayed his watches, and did whatever he could to make the passage more enjoyable. An avid racer, Rocky tirelessly trimmed the sails in a futile attempt to speed HERE AND NOW on her way. "This is a race," he would re-mind Roger and me, as we smirked at his constant adjustments.

Despite Rocky's best efforts, HERE AND NOW lagged behind the fleet in the light air and high pressure that stretched across the North Atlantic. Henry Scheel, famous for his shoal-draft cruisers, designed the Morgan 45 for commodious cruising. Not to be con-fused with the performance-oriented, Nelson-Marek-designed Morgan 45 that came along a few years later, Scheel's boat fea-tured a raised saloon, ample freeboard and, of course, shoal draft. She was solidly constructed, comfortable in port, and revered by her owner. But she wasn't fast. Motoring in light air was permit-ted by rally rules; however, every hour the engine was in gear would be added to your total time. Logging engine hours was based on the honor system, a system that we would later learn wasn't very honorable.

Roger is a wonderful storyteller and he regaled us every after-noon with stories from the small town where he grew up. "There are more characters per square inch in Pilot Mountain, North Car-olina, than anywhere in the world." From the cloddish antics of Coot Lafollick, a shady knife trader, to underhanded deals of mule trader Beadie McCormick, Rocky and I would laugh until our sides ached at Roger's tales. Then there was Mr. Whittaker, the richest man in town but also the cheapest. "One day," Roger explained, "old man Whittaker, who was so cheap that he tied his glasses to his ears so he didn't have to buy eyeglass frames, took his girlfriend to the county fair. After looking at everything but not buying anything, his frustrated girlfriend was mighty hungry. 'Oh Mr. Whittaker,' she cried out, 'don't those hot dogs smell good?'

" 'They sure do Missy,' old man Whittaker replied, 'why don't we move a little closer so we can smell 'em even better.' "

Gary, whose sense of humor was apparently more refined than the rest of us, would just roll his eyes, that is, if his eyes were open; for most of the time that he wasn't on watch he was sleeping. He was driving Roger crazy. Just to completely annoy Gary, Roger would insist on playing Frank Sinatra's 'My Way' at full volume every afternoon, with the requirement that the crew assemble on what we dubbed the fantail and sing along. Roger would personally wake Gary whenever he could. By flying the spinnaker and judiciously using our rapidly dwindling fuel supply, we reached the halfway point in seven days.

A few nights later, Roger bellowed, "Fire." Rocky later remarked, "It was a good thing nobody was in Bligh's way or we'd have had a few broken bones to contend with too." In a twisted response to the complete lack of discipline I required aboard, Roger and Rocky had taken to calling me Captain Bligh. Fire was a bit of an exaggeration, luckily, but the overheating engine was smoldering. I quickly noticed that the water pump belt was broken and without cooling water an engine will definitely overheat. Roger had plenty of spare belts but that wasn't the problem. Because we were dependent upon the generator and 110 volts for so many systems, Roger had installed an extra, belt-driven generator that ran off the main engine. Unfortunately, this huge contraption had to be mounted directly on top of the main engine and even the simplest task, like changing a belt, turned into a major project requiring the complete removal of the 'auto gen'. As you might imagine, a few choice curses were directed at the spare generator.

Autopilots and fuel gauges are the two most deceitful gadgets on any sailboat. The expensive Robertson autopilot and natty Gary had much in common, neither one worked, but an inaccurate fuel gauge caused the most grief. Confident that we had a sufficient amount of fuel, at least for a few more days, we were merrily motoring along on day 11 when the engine surged once and then suddenly stopped. That we were out of fuel never dawned on me and

I bled the system until my fingers were raw and the starter was fried before I realized what the problem was. The last five days of the passage were agonizingly slow as HERE AND NOW, and her extensive inventory of spare parts, which included everything but a starter, drifted eastward. Luckily, Frank Sinatra and crew from Pilot Mountain gave us inspiration to keep going.

Twenty miles from Horta, we sat completely becalmed. Rocky was miserable for the first time. His flight home was for the following day, and although we were pretty sure we would drift ashore by flight time, he was distraught that he might not have time for at least one cold Sagres at Café Sport. On the horizon I noticed a sailboat steaming toward Horta. "To hell with the TransArc," I told Roger. "It's more important for Rocky to have a beer at Café Sport." I swallowed my considerable pride and called the yacht's skipper. After a little groveling on my part, he reluctantly agreed to tow us into the harbor. The tow accomplished two things: first, Rocky had plenty of time to sample the local beverages; and second, happily, we were disqualified from the rally. Roger, in a remarkable show of spirit, attended the Rally party in Horta anyway. He accepted with quiet dignity the DNF (did not finish) for HERE AND NOW at the bottom of the race-results sheet, but he was miffed when a Hallberg-Rassy 42 was declared the leg winner in our class. The German-owned boat, which had scooted past us while we lay becalmed, apparently had actually been sailing even without any sails set. On the official results sheet they had logged zero hours of motoring.

Bobby Truett, another Winston-Salem friend, turned up in Horta loaded with replacement parts. We managed to fix everything during our brief stay and prepared for leg three, which, for some perverse reason, Roger was determined to finish with the rally fleet. On the morning before departure, the strained relationship between Roger and Gary reached an impasse. Roger had asked his first mate to hose down the boat and clean up underneath the cockpit grate. Gary thought this task was below him, and mumbled something about how the collected food under the grate represented a living history of the passage to date and was absolutely disgusting. Overhearing his snide comment, Roger looked me squarely in the eye. "Meet me on the foredeck," he announced and marched forward with steam rising from his ears.

"Captain," he said, "would you call me a reasonable man?"

"Of course, and what's with this captain stuff? It makes me nervous. Call me John, or at least Bligh."

"Captain," Roger was serious, "do you know what is tucked away under the navigation seat?"

"Yes, your 357 Magnum. Why?" Now I was nervous and remembered why I don't believe in guns aboard boats.

"Because I am going to give you two choices. You agreed I am a reasonable man."

"Okay. What are my choices?"

"You either fire that son of a bitch right here, right now, or I will shoot him."

"Roger!"

"Captain!"

I took choice A. I paid Gary off—I had actually negotiated a wage for him—and told him to pack his bags and be off the boat as quickly as possible. It was not a pretty sight as he ambled down the dock under the weight of his monogrammed, matching duffel bags.

Leg three was much more relaxed and finally both HERE AND NOW and the Atlantic weather performed as expected. Bobby Truett was so pleasant and so capable I wondered why Roger hadn't hired him to skipper the boat. Like Rocky and Penn, he was a great shipmate and became a treasured friend who would sail with me again. Roger and I had formed a close relationship throughout the course of the passage and we spent hours discussing philosophy. Although our natures are basically different, almost opposite, I admired his ability to look an issue in the eye and deal with it. He told me that the key to happiness is not to let others impose their will on you. He detested compromise and had no sympathy for those who lived "lives of quiet desperation," his favorite and oft-mentioned quote of Thoreau. I could not help but wonder, though, if Roger actually accomplished the ambitious sailing he planned during the next few years, that old King Neptune wouldn't force a little compromise down his throat.

The days raced by and it seemed extravagant not to steer all day and night. After a week, we sighted the massive gray rock of Gibraltar. The only complaints were with my cooking, especially a frozen shellfish paella that I'd stocked up on in Horta but served only once. A *vendavales*, a stiff local wind that haunts the straits, dusted us before we tied up at Marina Bay. My fourth crossing was complete. Despite our many problems, we had transited the Atlantic in 30 sailing days.

By the time Molly and I sailed into Fort Lauderdale, a year later, our relationship was essentially kaput and I was weary of cruising. I have never been one to putter about a boat and peacefully while away weeks at anchor. I like to sail. I longed for an adventure and, not to mention, needed some money. A quick visit to Joe's office produced both and before long I was consumed in the preparations of what would prove to be my most challenging and frustrating delivery ever. I had agreed, against all the collected wisdom and advice of my friends and colleagues, to deliver an 80-year-old, 74-foot teak ketch from Fort Lauderdale to Indonesia.

I turned down the delivery three times before finally caving in. My dear friend Steve Maseda shook his head when I told him that I had finally agreed to take the job, claiming that it was just too good of an opportunity to pass up. "Opportunity? Right, Kretschmer, you have round heels when it comes to deliveries, you're a pushover."

Steve was right but that was common knowledge; there was, however, more to my decision than just needing another delivery fix. I was intrigued by ISOLETTA, I liked and respected her new owners and, most importantly, I was challenged at the prospect of sailing across the Pacific in an old wooden ship. This was my most ambitious project since the Cape Horn gig.

The naysayers turned up like teredo worms. Boatyard workers told me of ISOLETTA's dubious recent history and a former skipper snidely remarked to make sure the liferaft inspection was current. I also had my own doubts. Observing the boat from a distance as she lay on the hard in a Fort Lauderdale boatyard, there was no hiding the hog of her sheerline and the droopiness of her stern. Much of her gear had, as they say in England, gone shoddy. Still, the overall picture was seductive. A classic, Fife-designed English pilot cutter, she was massively constructed in solid teak and built in Scotland in 1908. She had a stubby bowsprit, a North Sea bow, handsome bulwarks and long, flush teak decks. There was a small, elegant pilothouse and no real cockpit, just a beautiful spoked wheel, a helmsman seat and two cockpit benches well aft. Her thick spruce spars were off the former royal yacht BLOOD HOUND and supposedly her rig and sails were in good shape. She was full keeled and long legged, drawing about eight feet.

In some ways, ISOLETTA was like an eccentric old English dame whose long-ago royal connections were questionable and who had obviously been living for quite a while among commoners. Her interior, which you reached via a spiral staircase from the pilothouse, had once been elegant. But by the time I came to be her skipper, the dark mahogany panels and leaded glass cabinets gave the boat the aura of a seedy southcoast pub, with tired furnishings from the Victorian age. Old ISOLETTA was a classic that had fallen through the cracks and been owned by a succession of sailors who did not have enough money to dress her up for the ball. Yet, if you looked closely, there were still traces of nobility and proper breeding. In the end, you either had to walk away from her, acknowledging that she had fallen from grace, or accept her for what she used to be and, hopefully, might be again.

Karen, an American attorney and Tim, an Australian mining engineer, were an unlikely couple and even more unlikely owners of ISOLETTA. They lived in Djakarta and, like others from all over the world, came to Fort Lauderdale to buy a boat. They hooked up with Joe and after looking at several practical fiberglass boats, for some inexplicable reason made a hard left turn into la-la-land and bought ISOLETTA. Joe tried to talk them out of it. But when the survey revealed that, although she needed refitting and updating, all vital signs pointed to basic structural integrity, they went ahead and closed the deal. Originally they planned to ship her back to Indonesia, where labor was cheap and there was no shortage of wooden-boat skills. However, the cost was staggering and furthermore, nobody would even consider insuring the old girl if she rode along as deck cargo. Oddly, Lloyds was willing to bet on me and without much ado we obtained coverage to deliver her on her own bottom.

Karen and Tim had noble intentions and fully intended to restore ISOLETTA to her former glory once we reached Indonesia. In the meantime, we analyzed what was critical and what was cosmetic and began preparing for a 10,000-mile passage. We added new backstay chainplates and new spreaders. We also rigged up a Harken roller-furling system on the headstay and installed new electronics, including radar, SatNav and SSB. We overhauled the generator and the diesel, a 40-year-old Ford that, to my amazement, still snapped to life with just a little prodding. Looking back at our preparations, I cringe at how totally naive we were about the over-all condition of the hull.

Edd Kalehoff, my producer-composer friend, and his new bride Andrea McArdle skated down to the dock a few days before departure. Andrea, who was the original, adorable Annie on Broadway and in London, seemed a lot steadier than Edd, who I was afraid might skate right off the dock and into the drink. Andrea had just wrapped up starring in *Starlight Express*, a Broadway musical in which the cast performed on skates. Edd didn't like my suggestion that he wear a PFD whenever he laced up his skates. Edd owned a classic Sparkman and Stephens yawl, MAGIC VENTURE, and was a knowledgeable and enthusiastic wooden-boat sailor. Andrea was game for most anything and they signed on for leg one, Fort Lauderdale to Panama.

Finding a crew to complete the entire journey was a bit more challenging. Many people were intrigued by the prospect of sailing an old wooden ship across the Pacific but just couldn't find three or four months of spare time. I knew I needed a full-time engineer/mechanic to keep up with ISOLETTA's ancient systems. Scott Palmer is one of those rare people who can communicate with any kind of machinery by instinct, and make it do what it is supposed to do. He grew up fixing cars and then turned to boats. A licensed captain, Scotty was also a good friend and former teacher at my navigation school. Captain Bob Pierce, one of my dearest friends, also signed on for the voyage. A former merchant seaman, Bob spent most of his life building houses in New Jersey. After retiring to Florida, he started delivering boats and I knew him to be a fine sailor and the steadiest of hands. Bob was in his early 60s but was in great shape and his carpenter skills would surely prove useful. I still needed a cook. My mother, back from Alaska, had decided to join the Peace Corps. Fortunately, she had at least six months before posting, just enough time to make the long passage aboard ISOLETTA. I knew that she could cook in any conditions and I also had a premonition that her indomitable optimism would be a valuable commodity aboard.

A crowd of well-wishers saw us off from the outer dock at River Bend Marina. We also had many guests aboard for the long ride down the New River. The journey nearly ended before it began as I narrowly averted impaling a couple of tourists aboard the JUNGLE QUEEN with ISOLETTA's bowsprit. As we topped our tanks at the fuel dock, Ty Techera, who had made the ceremonial river ride, took me aside. He was concerned. "John, remember how badly this boat leaked on your sea trials last week. I know you thought it was the stuffing box but don't be blind to problems. Don't let your ego get the best of you. If this old boat can't make the trip, don't force her. No boat is worth dying for." Ty's cautionary words sent a chill down my spine.

I patted him on the shoulder and smiled. "Don't worry Ty, I'll go easy."

On May 2, 1989 we cleared Port Everglades. The east wind was gentle and the seas less than two feet, perfect conditions to begin a long voyage. Unfortunately, ISOLETTA was leaking like a Haitian sloop even in those light conditions. We had mounted a huge manual bilge pump on deck and once you built up a head of steam, the pump moved half a gallon of water per stroke; it was easy to monitor how much the boat leaked. She leaked 60 gallons the first hour, 90 the second and 100 gallons the third. Kalehoff, who knew more about wooden boats than the rest of us, was unnaturally pensive and genuinely concerned. We probed around the hull from below but there was not an obvious leak. She was weeping all over. "She'll take up," became my mantra, hoping that as the boat worked some saltwater into her soul, she would swell and the leaking would ease up.

A few miles off Key Largo, Kalehoff and I launched the dinghy and examined a few of the waterline butt blocks, the point where two plank ends are joined. Back in the boat, we mixed up some waterproof epoxy and smeared it into the butt-block seams. It did little to stem the leaking. I just didn't want to believe that ISOLETTA had serious problems and kept blindly assuring everyone, "She'll take up." Our first night at sea was uneventful but the leak steadily increased. Reluctantly, I decided to head for Key West; we were leaking 100 to 150 gallons every hour.

Although outwardly I was calm and confident, my subconscious reaction betrayed me. A popular song at the time was *She*

Drives Me Crazy, by a group called The Fine Young Cannibals. I am one of those obnoxious people who, despite being unable to carry a tune in a bucket, sings relentlessly, even in the face of unabated criticism. I hummed, whistled and sang this ditty, which certainly seemed appropriate, over and over. I couldn't get it out of my head. This particular song had a melodic part at the end of the refrain that required an "Oh, oh, oh." My version of "Oh, oh, oh" made Andrea shudder and I confess did not remotely resemble the Fine Young Cannibals' rendition. Andrea's disgust finally gave way to pity. "Are you really trying?" she would ask. I nodded, smiled and kept on singing. Indeed, "She drives me crazy" became my new delivery theme, especially as it became obvious that ISOLETTA was never going to take up.

In Key West Kalehoff explained why the boat was not taking up. "Wooden boats take up if they have been out of the water for a long time, but only for a few days after launching. Working a boat does not help it take up, it makes it worse." I knew this too but just didn't want to believe it. Edd urged us to have the boat hauled in Key West and have the hull surveyed again. I dreaded the delay, knowing that deliveries need momentum. If we could manage to pump our way to Panama, we would have a better feeling for what needing doing—and we would be far enough into the voyage where turning around would not be an easy option. I never doubted that I would deliver ISOLETTA to Indonesia and knew that the hard part was to get out of Florida first. Edd, Bob and I worked tirelessly, recaulking seams near the waterline and slathering epoxy over butt blocks. Scott tackled the electrical system, which had a mind of its own and was constantly acting up. Mom and Andrea topped off the provisions. On the afternoon of May 5 we cleared Key West, once again bound for Panama. Unfortunately, the brief delay spoiled the tight scheduling window for Edd and Andrea and they had to leave the boat in Key West. As a parting gift, Andrea gave me her Walkman, my very own Fine Young Cannibals tape and some advice: "Don't let this boat drive you crazy."

Our repairs seemed to help and the leak was down to a mere trickle, just 30 gallons an hour as we skirted Cabo San Antonio off the western tip of Cuba on a lovely reach. Another disappointing feature of ISOLETTA was her sailing performance, or lack thereof; she was a slug. In 15 to 20 knots, we lumbered along at five knots on a beam reach, this in a 74-foot boat with all canvass flying. I realized that when sailing off the wind the leak was manageable; however, as soon as we cleared Cuba and brought the boat hard on the wind, ISOLETTA resumed her voracious consumption of saltwater. ISOLETTA could not be sailed with the wind forward of the beam, not if you wanted to stay afloat for very long. The Yucatán Channel is notoriously rough and as we began slamming into short, choppy seas, we began leaking more than 200 gallons an hour. Reluctantly, I steered for Cozumel, a large island off the coast of Mexico and easily reached on a favorable point of sail.

It was obvious that something had to be done. ISOLETTA was not going to make it to Panama, much less across the Pacific. Still, I was determined not to abort the voyage and clung to the belief that ISOLETTA could be patched up to a point to allow us to continue. From the commodore of the Club Náutico in Cozumel I learned about a commercial shipyard on the island of Roatán in the Bay Islands of Honduras. I was assured that the railway lift there could handle ISOLETTA and that it would be an inexpensive and capable spot to enact repairs. Also, it was only 250 miles to the south, a direction that would most likely entail a reach in easterly tradewinds. I called Karen and Tim in Djakarta. They were appalled when I told them about the leaking problems and instructed me to take whatever action was prudent. I told them that my intentions were to have the boat repaired as necessary, which might involve a complete recaulking job, and then head for Panama. I tried to sound upbeat but doubt had crept into my brain. Fortunately, Karen and Tim trusted me completely, knowing that if it was possible to get the boat to Indonesia, I would find a way do it.

We cleared customs at Coxen Hole on the east end of Roatán before making our way to French Harbour. Unless they are unlucky enough to be part of the duty-free feeding frenzy of unleashed cruiseship passengers, small island ports in this age of air travel usually don't bother to dress up the seaward side of their waterfronts. And why should they, the tourists they're courting come by air and are quickly whisked away to a secluded resort. There is no need to expose them to the messy and fascinating wharfs. Traveling by sailboat, however, especially to countries that carry that dubious distinction of not being a member of the so-called First World, is most revealing. Anchored off Coxen Hole, I felt as if we

ISOLETTA being hauled up on a rickety railroad lift in Roatán in the Bay Islands of Honduras.

were sneaking up on the Bay Islands, entering through the back door. From the sporadically planked outhouses perched on the end of wobbly finger piers, to the noisy cranes off-loading an odd assortment of goods from the decks and holds of small rusty coasters, Coxen Hole had nothing to hide. Indeed, the Bay Islands are wonderfully confused as Spanish-speaking officials from the Honduran mainland try to rein in the fiercely independent, English-speaking islanders. I felt at home immediately.

ISOLETTA was, however, driving me crazy. On the gentle reach to Roatán she leaked less than 20 gallons an hour, a flow that we easily kept up with, a virtual trickle that spawned renewed hopes of easing our way across the Pacific. I had studied the pilot charts carefully and concluded that if we stayed near the Equator, we would avoid the doldrums, which lie just north of the line, and find favorable but light winds. I envisioned lining ISOLETTA's ample decks with spare fuel cans in Panama, and calculated that we could carry enough fuel to motor 3,000 of the 4,000 miles from the canal to Penrhyn Island, an atoll in the northern Cook Islands. Just as I was ready to skip past the Bay Islands with blind confidence, I came to my senses and remembered the steady stream of water that filled the bilge in any kind of a seaway.

In French Harbour we moored ISOLETTA alongside a half-sunk, rusty schooner, across the harbor from Seth Arch's dry dock.

A crusty but likable former seaman with a sing-song voice, Seth was from one of the islands most prominent families. Like many of the locals, he traced his roots back to the Cayman Islands. Unfortunately, we couldn't have picked a worse to time to arrive. The Bay Islands are home to one of the largest shrimp fleets in the world and May is the month when annual maintenance is done on the steel-hulled trawlers. It would be a couple of weeks at best, and possibly a month or more, before Seth could schedule us on the railway. Knowing the nature of tropical islands, I assumed the worst. I explained our frustrating dilemma to Seth, who like most seamen of his age, claimed to understand the mysteries of the universe and wooden boats. "I'll send a man down tomorrow. He's old but he's good. He'll dive on the boat, see what he can do."

The next morning, Eddy, a strapping black man from Nicaragua, turned up at the boat with scuba tank, a wad of caulking and a *big* hammer. Seth instructed him to look at the planking butts, check for any proud planks and wide seams. Then he disappeared into the water, pulling his tank behind him. Wham, Wham, Wham, he started hammering caulking into the seams. I was horrified, afraid that with one mighty blow he might sink the boat. But Eddy knew his business and he steadily worked his way around the huge hull, pounding caulking into every butt block. Bob and I followed his progress from below and were amazed; it was like turning off a faucet. By the time Eddy resurfaced, I was ecstatic and ready to push on for Panama.

It concerned me that Mom, who rarely worries about anything on a boat, was suspect of Eddy's repair job. Scotty also thought ISOLETTA would open up again as soon as we worked her in any kind of sea. Bob probably felt the same way but he wanted to sail across the Pacific as much as me and kept his doubts to himself. On May 17 we set off for Panama, yet again, and this time made it the all way to Port Royal, 15 miles away on the east end of Roatán. The easterlies had begun to pipe up, near 30 knots, and I didn't want to sink my fragile optimism on the first day.

Port Royal is one of the most beautiful natural harbors in the Caribbean. It reminded me of Virgin Gorda Sound, except for the fact that ISOLETTA had the vast anchorage to herself. We met Eric Anderson and his delightful family, who lived a fantasy life in a beautiful home made of local hardwoods overlooking the harbor.

Eric, an expatriate, discovered the Bay Islands when he worked for Cessna in the 60s. He sold and delivered small planes to Central American dictators and from the air marveled at the majesty of the Bay Islands. Eric eventually landed on Roatán and, together with his father, invested in property all over the island. I didn't know it at the time but Eric and I would become great friends and sail together often. It would have been easy to while away many days on Eric's cool, book-lined veranda but my mind was in Panama. I just knew that if we could make it to Panama, we could make it across the Pacific.

The tradewinds pile up in the western Caribbean, 25- to 35-knot easterlies are not uncommon in the Bay Islands. I couldn't wait any longer; it was time to test Eddy's repair. We motored out of Port Royal and struggled to reef the main. ISOLETTA was a cumbersome boat to handle and the roller-reefing system for the mainsail bordered on the ridiculous. It seemed like a hundred turns of the small worm gear equaled a single turn of the boom. Also, it was always an adventure moving from the security of the pilothouse back to the exposed cockpit benches. You had to wait for a steady moment and then dash aft and clutch the mizzen mast. We lumbered southeast, hoping to clear Cabo Gracias a Dios, a headland on the border between Honduras and Nicaragua. Good old Christopher Columbus named this headland in a humble moment. From the Bay Islands, a distance of 200 miles, it took him 28 days to beat around the cape! No wonder that was his fourth and final voyage.

An hour out of Port Royal, we finally had ISOLETTA trimmed. We were flying the main with a deep reef, the mizzen with a single reef, the staysail and about half of the yankee. We were kicking up sheets of spray, thundering to weather in 30 knots of breeze and making all of six knots. I sympathized with Columbus, as I dropped below to check the bilge. While it took a moment for my eyes to adjust to the darkness of the cabin, my ears and feet knew instantly that we were sinking. Green water was sloshing two feet above the cabin sole and the level was rising. I flew on deck and hollered at Bob and Scott to come about, giving particular emphasis to the word NOW! We came crashing through the wind and dropped all sail save the mizzen and staysail. Then we rigged up the emergency, gas-powered trash pump, which I had purchased just for this occasion. I gave a silent prayer of thanks when, by some miracle, it started on the third pull and the 2-inch hose immediately began sucking water out of the boat. We had two large electric pumps working and I stroked the manual pump for all I was worth. Running before the wind, ISOLETTA's leaks eased up a bit, while we neared Port Royal. We were more than breaking even. Our quick efforts spared ISOLETTA a watery grave.

There was nothing to do but wait for Seth Arch to haul the old girl. In the meantime, we secured the boat at the French Harbour Yacht Club docks. The club, owned in part by Eric Anderson, was an oasis of peace and quiet in bustling, dusty, dirty French Harbour. I was depressed. It was obvious that ISOLETTA's 80-year-old hull needed a lot of help. When she finally made her way up the rickety railroad lift, it was far worse than I imagined. ISOLETTA's massive construction had seduced and then deceived us all. She was impressively fastened with bronze bolts securing 1½-inch teak planks to husky, sawn-oak frames. However, as we pulled several fasteners, we learned that even if the head of the bolt and nut appeared perfect, the barrel of the bolt was completely corroded on the inside. Also, many of the robust teak planks were actually honeycombed with rot despite appearing sound on both edges. The

ISOLETTA on the hard in Roatán.

more we dug, the more serious the problems became. It was clear that electrolysis was the culprit. Once the caulking was reamed out, I could reach my fingers between some seams and literally pull planks off the hull. Throughout this process, I was in constant communication with Karen and Tim, who were coming to realize that they were the proud owners of a rotten ship.

I stopped the work in midstream as I had a terrible vision of ISOLETTA dying on the hard in French Harbour, Roatán. It was apparent to me that Seth's crew did not have the skills or the materials to put ISOLETTA in shape. I called Karen and Tim one more time and strongly recommended that we forego the delivery, at least for the time being. The only solution was to piece the boat back together, nurse her to Florida and have a proper and complete repair done at a competent yard. "I have two critical questions," Tim said. "First, I don't want you to risk your life or the life of your crew. This is serious. Do you really think you can get the boat back to Lauderdale? And if the answer to the first question is yes, then how much do you think a proper repair will cost?"

I took a deep breath. "The answer to the first question is: probably. We'll do what's necessary here in Roatán and take it easy. It's only 800 miles," I said, trying to sound hopeful. "As far as the cost goes, Tim, I'm not sure, but my guess is not less that 50,000 Dollars and possibly a lot more. We owe Seth nearly 8,000 Dollars already and that's just for a partial caulking job and a few new planks." I could hear Tim swallow hard on the end of the line and could almost taste the bitterness in his throat. A gentleman to the core, he thanked me sincerely for staying with the boat despite the many problems. "If you think the boat can make it back, then that's the best plan of action but don't take any unnecessary risks." Karen wondered if she needed to send more money and I told her that I had enough left from my advance to pay the yard bill and that we'd settle up our accounts in Florida.

Seth Arch suggested that we copper over all the seams below the waterline. Ty Techera flew down from Fort Lauderdale with a couple of huge rolls of copper strips and we set about nailing them to the hull. Ty, who is fearless and loves adventures, also agreed to help Scotty and me bring the boat home. "I don't want you to have all that fun in the liferaft," he quipped when I picked him up at the tiny airport. Bob and Mom had run out of time. Both had been stalwart crew members and were just as disappointed as I was that the Pacific voyage never materialized.

With as much metal as wood on the bottom and benevolent winds and seas, we sailed back to Fort Lauderdale in five days. Nothing was ever stress-free on ISOLETTA and news of a tropical storm heading toward Florida made the last couple of days a bit tense, but luckily it veered north. I guided ISOLETTA into the same slip we had left two months earlier. As I lashed a spring line to a stout piling, I was filled with a strange mixture of disappointment, anger and melancholy. ISOLETTA was the first boat that I had failed to deliver to its destination.

*   *   *

"These must be the reverse tradewinds," Lesa remarked snidely, as SIREN'S SONG was forced to beat into a biting north wind. "Didn't you promise me east winds, what was that big chart you showed me back in Boca Chita, a pilot chart I think you called it? Well, Capitán Norteamericano, I think you should throw it overboard. Of course, after the ISOLETTA disaster, I guess I shouldn't complain, at least we're not sinking. So what happened? I have a terrible feeling that you did not get paid very well for all your trouble."

"How did you know that?"

"It's pretty obvious that you'd rather be noble than rich."

"For your information, the estimates to properly refasten and replank the hull were staggering. Tim came to the States and worked side by side with a shipwright and they did a wonderful job of putting the boat back in shape.

"Unfortunately, when it came time to have her delivered, he and Karen were out of money. Tim tackled the job himself but he just didn't have the experience for a long ocean passage. The last I heard, he left the boat in Panama and as far as I know she may still be sitting there. In fact, I did see her there the next year when I took a boat to Costa Rica. It's a shame."

"What a sad story. Promise me you'll never buy a wooden boat."

"That's one promise I'll make and keep."

"So by the way, what about the money? They must have owed you a pile?"

"I didn't have the heart to ask for any more money. They had enough problems and I did make a bit of money, not much though. Okay, I admit it, I didn't make much at all, almost nothing for three months of working my ass off. In fact, I was pretty well tapped out when we got back to Lauderdale. But I quickly rounded up another delivery. You see, there was this ornery red schooner that needed to be taken to France and, well, that's the next story for you, after you round up two more Presidentes."

Lesa shook her head and smiled. "Well, nobody will accuse me of marrying you for your money."

CHAPTER 8

Just Another Crossing

You long without doubt to know how, after having been ship-wrecked five times, and escaped so many dangers, I could resolve again to tempt fortune, and expose myself to new hard-ships. I am, myself, astonished at my conduct when I reflect upon it, and must certainly have been actuated by my destiny. But be that as it may, after a year's rest I prepared for a sixth voyage, notwithstanding the entreaties of my kindred, who did all in their power to dissuade me.

SINBAD, before his sixth voyage, The Arabian Nights

THE CHUNKY RED SCHOONER that everybody assumed was built of ferro-cement was undeniably ugly. I don't say that easily. I've been called a sailboat whore and it is true, I love them all: the good, the bad, even the ugly. I am sailing's Lothario; there is no boat that can resist my charms (except ISOLETTA); I can deliver any boat, from world class yachts to reluctantly afloat hulks. For better and sometimes worse, no boat can remain idle after I come to know her. Standing on the dock, sipping a beer with Joe, I surveyed the lumpy teak decks and peeling paint of TAI O HAE.

"Okay, Joe, what's the story? You know after ISOLETTA you owe me a nice trip and this," I said, pointing at the boat, which also had a disturbing port list, "does not look like a nice trip."

"You told me you needed money. I found you a boat to de-liver. What can I say, John? I don't think she's quite as bad as she looks. Besides, it's just another crossing. Be thankful she's not wood."

I couldn't help but laugh. Joe knew me too well. He knew that I would agree to deliver the old heap and he didn't need to sell me on the job; we were just going through the protocol, the mating dance. Also, I needed to redeem myself for what I perceived as profound failure with the ISOLETTA project. It was a comeuppance for me to realize that sometimes sheer will alone will not prevail in a three-way duel with a leaky ship and Neptune. An edge, no doubt a healthy edge, had been shaved off my cockiness. Chalky red redemption, leaning precariously to port, floated before me. I got back to the protocol.

"How long has she been on the market, Joe? Why do they want her back in France all of a sudden?"

"I've had her listed for three years without a single offer. She's owned by a nice old couple who think she is worth a lot more than she really is. Maybe in France she is worth something. But here, she's an ugly boat full of idiosyncrasies and just doesn't appeal to the typical American looking for a cruising boat. But the old couple, and they are really quite nice for frogs, have sailed her all over the world. She's even named after some island in the Marquesas that they tell me is quite beautiful."

"Stop it, Joe, I'll start crying soon. By the way, maybe that's why you couldn't sell her. You had the wrong information. Tai O Hae is actually a village on the island of Nuka Hiva. Anyway, what will they pay?"

"The usual, 10 grand, all in. Can you do it for that?"

"Ya, I can do it for that."

That I decided to deliver TAI O HAE across the Atlantic instead of taking a job as the full-time skipper of a Hatteras 65 motorsailer demonstrated to many, even friends and family that should have known better, that I was dangling on the edge of reality, that maybe I was too far out there, I just wasn't growing up after all and really was flirting with mermaids. The Hatteras owner was much too corporate for my tastes; and although he offered a good salary and benefits, I wanted no part of the job. He was incredulous that I turned down his offer and commented, after I asked him about the nature of his work, "You ask too many questions for a boat captain." He looked very nautical and wore a belt and hat with signal flags, although he had no idea what they meant. I had a lovely idea to have a custom belt made for him with signal flags that spelled out something like . . . Well, I'll leave that to your imagination.

That fact that two French delivery crews had been dispatched to fetch TAI O HAE and failed only increased my hubristic desire to sail her across the pond.

The first skipper, who was obviously a sensible person, took one look at the boat and caught the next flight back to France. The next year another crew made it from Fort Lauderdale to Palm Beach before they gave up in despair. When I asked Joe what the problems were, he vaguely mentioned something about the engine and assured me that "a lot of work was being done to make the boat fit for the crossing."

I was, at this time, writing frequently for the yachting press and had become a contributing editor for *SAILING* Magazine. The editor, Micca Hutchins, was intrigued at how I made my living delivering boats all over the world and published most of my delivery pieces. When she passed through Fort Lauderdale a week before I planned to set sail I took her over to see TAI O HAE. Micca helped survey the boat when she nearly fell through a rotten section of foredeck we had yet to discover. Back on the dock she had a better-you-than-me look on her face and suggested, without cracking a smile, "that there might be a story in this crossing."

The owners had commissioned my friend Jerry, a skilled shipwright and mechanic, to go over TAI O HAE's systems. Jerry worked furiously under the scorching early summer sun, rebuilding the decks with plywood, changing out a few frozen seacocks and servicing the Perkins diesel. Despite his occasional outbursts of "I hate this . . .ing boat" and "Kretschmer, you're out of your . . .ing mind to even think about sailing this piece of shit across the Atlantic," he promised me that the boat would be ready before hurricane season kicked in. I was faced with the age-old dilemma of rounding up crew, although by all accounts, it was much easier to shanghai people in the olden days. Fortunately, Molly, who afterwards blamed temporary insanity, agreed to make the passage as we were once again trying to make our unusual but devoted relationship work. Insurance required a third crew man and my usual assortment of sailing cronies all remembered prior commitments after seeing the boat. Finally, I enlisted the services of my nephew.

Mike had recently graduated from college and was eager for a little adventure before starting graduate school in the fall and, with
a splendid show of Corinthian spirit, was willing to work for a refreshingly low wage.

On the way from the airport I tried to prepare Mike for his
first glimpse of TAI O HAE, but the expression on his face, the I-
can't-kill-you-because-you're-my-uncle look, told the story. But
Mike is a good kid, well raised by my sister, and instead of slugging
me or catching a taxi back to the airport, he smiled and said, "Well,
she looks strong, Uncle John," and then added, "It's a good thing
my mom and dad haven't seen the boat."

I patted him on the back and agreed cheerfully, "Oh, she is
strong, Mike, just tread gingerly on the decks, Jerry has not finished rebuilding them yet." Mike was puzzled when Molly told
him to stow his gear forward and handed him a box of plastic trash
bags. "I'd suggest you double bag anything you want to take home
again," she advised cynically, "just in case it rains."

Whack! "Oh, Mike, mind the SatNav." The owners of the
boat were either midgets or had a very perverse sense of humor.
For a 50-foot boat there wasn't much headroom to begin with but
to make matters worse they had mounted the largest, oldest-look-
ing electronic instruments at forehead height throughout the boat.
Stepping forward, you were sure to leave an impression of your
temple on the SatNav. Going aft was dangerous because an enormous radar screen hung menacingly in the walkway. If you stood
up abruptly from the chart table, you would see stars without a sextant from the blow issued by a massive black box that housed an
RDF that looked like it was made by Marconi. What made these
electronic assaults even more aggravating was that none of the
aforementioned navigational wizards worked.

We loaded our provisions aboard as Jerry removed his tools.

"What do you say, Jerry?" I asked, looking for encouragement.

"Shit, I don't know. The big red tub might make it across."

Not a stirring recommendation from a man who had just
spent a month working on the boat. A small group of friends
came down to see us off and, as we were bound for France,
couldn't resist shouting all the French phrases they knew as we
powered away from the dock. Fifteen minutes after we cleared
Port Everglades, the engine temperature gauge was reading 230

degrees, which was about 50 degrees too many. The sea was placid. Only the long undulating swells of the silent Gulf Stream reminded us that we were on the ocean. Eventually a light northerly breeze emerged and although we realized that in light air TAI O HAE sailed like cold molasses running uphill, we decided to press on. The Gulf Stream carried us north through the night but after hours in the engine room, I concluded that we needed to rebuild the cooling system. Time is money in the delivery business and the prospect of crossing the ocean without an engine was not a profitable one. We detoured to Port Canaveral and with a combination of luck and good seamanship, sailed into the dock without a scratch or scream.

Mike and I installed a new thermostat, rebuilt the water pump, and flushed out the heat exchanger. Twenty-four hours later we were back at sea. TAI O HAE was certainly an unusual boat. Her hull was fiberglass, layed up over an iron framework and the decks were plywood with teak over. She was strong, but she needed a modest gale to move. Also, the compass was erratic and despite my efforts to correct it, it had an error of around 30 degrees on most easterly headings. Still, the weather was light and we were making decent progress, motorsailing toward Bermuda, the first waypoint on the well-worn path across the Atlantic, which also included a call in the Azores.

Although schooner-rigged, TAI O HAE's sail plan was easy to handle and if there was a breeze, rather efficient. The mainsail was conventional with slab reefing but the foresail was a roller-furled fisherman. The staysail was hanked on and the high-cut yankee was roller-furled. The spinnaker was easy to set from the foremast and had a sock for hoisting and dousing. The weather turned squally and the diesel fickle on day three. We had a wild midnight retrieval of the spinnaker when a black cloud bank arrived with 40 knots of wind and it was becoming necessary to bleed the engine before every starting. But these annoyances would seem trivial by the next afternoon.

We were about halfway between Bermuda and the mainland, roughly 400 miles offshore, motoring again in light air when Molly noticed an odd clanking sound coming from the aft cabin. I hurried below. Oh no, not this again! The aft cabin floorboards were awash; we were leaking in a big way. I hollered for her to shut down the engine and frantically tossed the floor-boards out of the way. At first I thought it was just a monumental stuffing box leak, but then I noticed the stuffing box was riding halfway up the shaft. The bronze stern tube, or as it's sometimes called, the shaft log, which is the structural member that supports the stuffing box and cutless bearing, had cracked in two. Water was pouring in through a two-inch hole around the shaft.

I was calm; in fact, I told Mike that I was a leak specialist and that as long as he kept pumping the manual pump, there was nothing to worry about, at least for the moment. Naturally, the electric pump, which had been working fine previously, sputtered to a stop when we really needed it. I stuffed towels and rags around the shaft and instructed Molly to mix up a batch of underwater epoxy, which I carried just for this occasion. Molly handed me the goop and then instinctively flicked on the VHF radio and tried to make contact with any vessel. Naturally, we had the ocean to ourselves. I smeared the epoxy into the hole but it was difficult to keep in place. As advertised, it set up fast in just a few minutes, but it did nothing to stem the flow. Mike, who had a view of the situation from a port next to the pump in the cockpit, asked casually, "Uncle John, now would you say that we're sinking?"

I actually had to think about it before answering, "Yes, Mike, I think you could say that and we'd better do something about it pretty fast."

Mike and I quickly donned masks and dove overboard. We wrapped the shaft with plastic bags and strapped them down with bungy cords. Mike, a champion swimmer and strong of lung, made two dives to every one of mine and we managed to dramatically slow the leak. Back aboard, we added more epoxy from inside and rebuilt the electric pump. Then we waited for wind. I had decided that we would head for the nearest landfall based on the wind direction. When a southwester sprang up, Bermuda beckoned. Our makeshift repair held, although, just to be sure, Mike and I dove on it every six hours until the wind freshened as we approached Bermuda. Piling on sail and taking turns on the pump and with the buckets, we charged down narrow Town Cut into St. George's Harbour. We were really leaking badly and had formed a bucket brigade because the damned electric pump failed again. I suggested that Mike take a brief 10-second pause to gaze at the lovely pastel cottages dotting the hillsides. "That's okay, Uncle John, I'll see it on the way back out, and if there is not a way back out, I'll read your article for a description."

We sailed the boat directly into the haul-out slip at Bermuda Shipyard, once again doing an amazing job of it. Sailing to a dock is much easier if you don't spend much time thinking about it beforehand. The yard manager was furious and ordered us to move out.

"You don't have an appointment," he screamed.

"Sorry, old boy," I announced mockingly, "but if you don't haul us out in the next few minutes, you will be hauling us off the bottom."

Once the yard manager realized I was serious, he became reasonable and soon TAI O HAE was safely propped up ashore. I contacted the owners directly in Paris and spoke to Madame Richardson. Although obviously an older lady, her voice was lovely, and seductive. "Oh, Jean," she said softly as only a French woman can, "we appreciate all your hard work. You know my husband, he is ill, but he too appreciates all that you and your crew are doing to bring our precious boat home. Oh, Jean, Jean, Jean, you are such a good man. And your book, Jean, Joe sent it to me with your résumé, it is fantastic. It is so much more than a boating book. It reminds me of Camus, so powerful. We are so sorry about the problems with the boat. Just tell us how much the yard bill is and I will cable you the necessary funds."

Madame Richardson had me under a spell. Although Mike and I were beginning what would become three days of brutal labor, it didn't matter; I would take a bullet for Madame Richardson. This obviously brilliant, charming woman had actually compared me to Camus.

The first task was simply to remove the shaft, but the bolts holding the shaft to the transmission coupling refused to budge. We hammered them, we heated them, we cursed them, finally we cut them by hand with a hacksaw. Then, it was time to remove the old stern tube. Nothing short of nuclear explosives would have pried it from the boat, so we decided to sleeve it with a new piece of metal instead. Of course, there was nowhere on the island to

purchase thin-walled bronze, 1¹⁵⁄₁₆-inch in diameter. We had two
choices: incur additional delays and order piping from the States,
or head for the dumps.

The yard manager, who now sympathized with our noble
struggle, suggested that we rent scooters and scour the three large
garbage dumps on the island. He advised us to look for a certain
Allan Martin, the island junkman, who supposedly haunted the
dumps, hoarding the prime scrap. I envisioned Fred Sanford. Mike
and I charged off toward the first dump just outside of St. George's.
We encountered a rather scruffy individual and I asked if he was Mr.
Martin. He looked at me as if I was crazy and responded in the
Queen's English,

"Oh no, you mean the Scrap Chap. But I'm sorry he is not
here this morning, he's golfing."

It seemed odd that the junkman or, as he was also called, the
Scrap Chap would be golfing, especially on one of the world's most
expensive islands. I had just paid four dollars for a cup of coffee and
could only imagine what a round of golf would cost. After searching fruitlessly through the scrap metal, we continued on to the second dump near Hamilton. Again we stumbled into the perfect
stereotype of an island junkman. I asked him if he was Mr. Martin.
"Oh, no, you mean the the Scrap Chap. Sorry old boy but he's not
here, he's golfing." Mike and I looked at each other and laughed,
the Scrap Chap was obviously golfing.

"When do you think he'll be finished?"

"Oh, after lunch. You might find him at the dump near the old
fort in Somerset, but then again he might go to tea first."

After lunch we hurried to the third dump. Once again, we saw
a man organizing piles of scrap and figured that we had finally discovered the Scrap Chap.

"Good afternoon, sir," I said cheerfully. "You must be the
Scrap Chap."

The man looked at his watch and shook his head, "Oh no, the
Scrap Chap is at tea."

Exasperated we looked through the dump, measuring any
piece of metal tubing that looked close to the right size, but nothing fit. Depressed, we started home. About halfway back to the
boat, we came upon a small fabrication shop called Ornamental
Ironworks. Mike spied an old swimming pool ladder in the back of

the shop. It fit our dimensions to a T and the proprietor happily cut us a section just the right length. My excitement was tempered by the thought of how much that 8-inch piece of stainless steel was going to set me back. "How much," I asked softly, bracing for a Bermudian price.

"There is no charge, boys. You look like you've had a long day and I was going to give that old ladder to the Scrap Chap anyway."

Naturally, fitting the sleeve into the old stern tube and making sure it stayed in place was no small task. Although Mike was a philosophy major, he had scored a perfect 800 on the math section of the SAT test and he had an engineering mind. He supplied the concepts and I supplied the power. After another couple of days of working in the cramped bilge compartment of the aft cabin, we had the boat back together. One week after we arrived in Bermuda, we launched TAI O HAE and set sail for the Azores.

It seemed like we missed the Atlantic weather window by that very week. We sailed into a nasty black squall on day one and endured rainy squally weather for the next two weeks. It was well into July and I could just feel a tropical depression in the air. I even made up a little song. Luckily, all that I can remember is the refrain, which went, "I've got a tropical depression, the breeze is starting to freshen, I should have learned old Neptune's lesson before I got this damned depression," and then there was a little, "hmm, hmm, hmm" at the end.

It took the winds a week to clock around to the west and then, of course, they went light. As the wind died, an evil demon seemed to come alive aboard TAI O HAE and made mischief with our already jury-rigged systems. First, the iron fuel tanks began disintegrating and we had to redesign a fuel system using a plastic jerry can in the cockpit that gravity fed to a day tank in the engine room. Unfortunately, the cockpit tank only held about 6 gallons and every four hours needed 500 strokes of a manual pump from inside the sweltering engine room to maintain a prime. Next, the hydraulic steering system developed a leak. We bled the steering system constantly but the best that we could manage was 12 complete turns from lock to lock. Yes, you guessed it, the autopilot was the next to go and with the small, bulkhead-mounted wheel, steering became a miserable chore as

At the helm of TAI O HAE with the dramatic summit of Pico ahead.

the helmsman was constantly turning the wheel and, more often than not, wildly oversteering. Another nice feature was that the engine exhaust blower exited into the cockpit and was aimed precisely for the helmsman's face. Finally, the engine starter gave way, rendering the diesel useless, which was just as well; at least the person at the helm could breathe.

Mike was amazed that so many systems could fail so quickly. "Well, Mike," I reassured him, "this is pretty typical delivery fare and that's why my motto is, 'When something breaks, figure out why you never really needed it in the first place'." At cocktail hour, we discussed our favorite design flaws and placed bets on what system would fail next.

Eventually the verdant peaks of Faial decorated the distant horizon. We were treated to a lovely late-afternoon view of Pico piercing the cloud layer and saluting us from above. I had taken the starter to bits and tinkered with it for days. When I managed to jolt the engine to life for our arrival I felt like Rudolf Diesel reincarnated. It seemed luxurious to enter a harbor under power and we made our way to the customs quay just before dark. Not long after, a small sloop rafted alongside. The boat was registered in Bermuda and Mike and I chatted with the solo skipper.

"So, what do you do in Bermuda?" I asked.

"This may sound strange," he replied, somewhat embarrassed, "but I'm the island garbage man."

Mike and I looked at each with amazement. It couldn't be. I blurted out, "Don't tell me you're the Scrap Chap?"

"No," said the garbage man, "but we golf together."

Our initial plan was to spend just a few days in Horta, to make up for lost time in Bermuda. I knew exactly where to take the starter to be rewound and after a few beers at Café Sport and maybe a glass or two of the new Pico wine, the *vinho verde*, we would shove off for the English Channel. Waiting for the starter, Mike and I worked on the autopilot, which miraculously worked perfectly when we reassembled it. Two days later we installed the

Installing the starter. Ha, the glamorous life of a delivery skipper!

shiny, rebuilt starter. The engine cranked beautifully; it cranked its little heart out in fact but it refused to start. By necessity, I have become a decent diesel mechanic and I tried all my tricks for conning the engine to start. When they all failed we brought in the so-called professionals. The combined mechanical brain trust of all of Horta's engineers could not convince the Perkins to rumble to life. Officially, we concluded that the fuel-injection pump was the culprit but I suspect it was really the curse of the TAI O HAE.

At this point, we were all ready to abandon ship. The delivery had gone beyond the call of duty and who knew what misadventures lurked on the final 1,500-mile leg to Dieppe on the Normandy coast. Molly and Mike urged me to call the owners, not only to insist that they send a new injection pump immediately but also to demand more money for all of our hard work. I squirmed; I'm not good at asking for money, especially after I have made a deal. In my book, a deal is a deal, even a bad deal. Molly was adamant, "You could threaten to walk away from the boat," she said. "This is crazy. You didn't contract to rebuild the boat while delivering it." By the time I placed the call I was quite agitated. Molly and Mike were right, I should at least charge extra for lost time, if nothing else. Again, Madame Richardson answered the phone. That voice, that beautiful voice, at once she began to cast her magical spell. "Oh, Jean, Jean, captain, oh, Jean my captain, I am so glad you called. How is the voyage going?"

"I hate to be the messenger of bad news. It isn't my nature to complain," I hemmed and hawed, gradually revealing some of our problems but downplaying their seriousness, nothing that dashing Captain Camus couldn't handle. I told her about the injection pump and she was respectfully aghast. She told me her son would send a new one promptly. Before I could broach the delicate subject of money, however, she told me how her husband was fading fast and how she hoped that seeing the boat, his beloved TAI O HAE, might be the medicine his doctors could not prescribe. "We'll see you in France soon, my captain, no?"

What could I say but, "Yes, Madame."

"She must have sent it by sailboat," Mike lamented as we waited impatiently for the pump to arrive. Finally after a week we

On the dock at the marina in Horta. Maybe I should find a real job.

learned that the pump had been sent to Horta but was returned to Lisbon because it had not been specifically marked for a "yacht in transit." Nobody seemed to know how long it would take to clear up the paperwork problem. Mike could wait no longer. He had to be home for the start of classes and, like the arrival of the pump, there was also no way to predict how long it might take us to sail to Dieppe.

During our long stay at the pleasant marina in Horta, we came to know Swedish sailors Christer Leferdahl, his lovely wife Annika Ottander, and their new baby Jonathan. They were out of money, waiting for a wire transfer, which must have been on the same boat as our injection pump. Christer and I became instant friends. We looked at the world from the same angle and spent hours at Café Sport and other small cafés telling sea stories and planning future adventures. It is hard to tell when a casual acquaintance will dramatically change your life but meeting Christer would lead to a wonderful friendship and to the film project in the Western Caribbean a few years later. This, of course, would lead to my chance meeting of Lesa, which would lead to an entire new chapter in my life. Following that chain of events, one could say that a faulty fuel-injection pump was a very fortuitous failure in my life. But it sure didn't seem that way at the time. The news from Lisbon was not good. While the paperwork had been cleared up, the pump had disappeared. It was lost, a 1,200 Dollar injection pump was simply lost, floating in an abyss somewhere between Horta and Lisbon. I was furious and decided that Molly and I would sail the last leg. TAI O HAE was, after all, a sailboat and I arranged for a tow out of the harbor.

We had a new destination, Falmouth, England. Madame Richardson's son would meet us there and complete the voyage. I anticipated an 8- to 10-day passage and we slowly made our way north, hoping to pick up the prevailing westerlies. Without a means of charging the batteries, we hoarded our precious amps, which meant that we couldn't use the repaired autopilot. The pilot chart assured me that by latitude 42 north we'd have steady Force 4 or 5 westerlies. We had Force 3 from the northeast. An incessant routine of four hours of steering and four hours of sleeping left us 500 miles from the English coast after a week at sea. At latitude 48 north I was sure the westerlies would kick in and we would have a glorious reach down the channel. Instead the light winds clocked to the east, more headwinds. We held long tacks, 12 hours, but our progress was abysmal and in four full days we managed to make only 208 miles toward our destination. We were averaging two stinking knots!

Three mornings in a row we sailed into dense fog. Of course, we had no lights which made the eerie resonance of passing foghorns even more unnerving. We tried to stay clear of the major shipping lanes but there is just too much traffic pouring in and out the channel to keep clear of all traffic. One morning we heard a distinct wail of a foghorn that was obviously close. We strained our eyes for a glimpse of the ship and I responded with a toot of our meager air horn, which Molly claimed she could barely hear from the bow. When we heard the rumble of the ship's engines I was filled with rage. What could I do? In the light air it would take about a week to bring TAI O HAE through the wind. Then I had an inspiration, a message from some god. I dashed below, turned on the radar. I had a powerful notion that it was going start transmitting. What in the hell was I thinking? It made a horrible screeching sound, started to smoke, and emitted noxious purple fumes.

As the easterlies continued, I pleaded with the ocean to give us a break. I even promised to find a real job when we returned home. I studied the pilot chart for hours but when fish scale clouds and a falling barometer failed to produce a wind change on our 16th day out of Horta, I hit the wall. In a short, bitter ceremony in the cockpit, I torched the August pilot chart of the North Atlantic and sent it off to Valhalla. That must have been the sacrifice Neptune was looking for because later that day the westerlies arrived with a vengeance.

At the first sign of favorable winds, I popped up the spinnaker. I kept it up as the winds hit 15 knots. It seemed okay when the winds piped up to 20 knots; we were screaming toward Falmouth. With the winds at 25 knots, I knew it was time to drop the chute. By the time I reached the foredeck, the winds were at 30 knots. I pulled and pulled on the downhaul, trying to corral the billowing sail in the sock. I managed to force the sock down about 10 feet, swallowing the head of the chute. Then, for some idiotic reason, I wrapped the thin downhaul line around

Burning the pilot chart and sacrificing it to the Gods as TAI O HAE labors toward Falmouth.

my hand and pulled for all it was worth as Molly did her best to blanket the chute with the main. It started to collapse before a sudden gust filled the spinnaker again. The sock shot up and so did I, my hand trapped in the downhaul. I was spinnaker flying, something you don't usually do underway. Luckily, the sock ripped to shreds and I toppled to the deck with nothing bruised but by my ego.

"I think we'll leave the chute up for awhile," I said to Molly back in the cockpit. TAI O HAE actually hit 8 knots as we skidded toward Falmouth. I didn't care if the spinnaker exploded. I kept it up through the night although the winds were steady at 25 to 30 knots. The next morning the English coastline was in view. By noon we had made our way past the Lizard. In the early afternoon, we thundered right into Falmouth Harbour, the colorful spinnaker still pulling us along like huskies before a sled. We sped through the moored boats in the outer harbor. Finally, only 50 yards from the customs barge, we rounded up. The spinnaker flogged madly as I let the halyard fly and it toppled harmlessly to the deck. We unrolled the fisherman and eased alongside the barge as if we were sailing a Laser. It was, no doubt, TAI O HAE's finest hour and thankfully our last aboard that unmerciful slave ship.

Later that night we were having dinner at the elegant Greenbank Hotel, which not only overlooks the harbor but is also where Kenneth Grahame wrote *The Wind in the Willows*. While we all know the Water Rat's feelings about boats, I confess I was ready at that moment for a few days in Toad Hall. However, soon I was back in Falmouth Harbour, reliving our arrival and I couldn't help but laugh out loud when I overheard the conversation at a nearby table.

"I've never seen anything like it," a stiff-necked gentleman in a tweed jacket explained to his companion.

"Dead right," his companion agreed, stroking the five or six hairs that he stretched completely over his head.

"It was either the best seamanship I've ever seen or the most reckless. I haven't quite decided. Imagine sailing a boat that size through this crowded harbor under spinnaker in that wind. Really quite remarkable."

"Yes, well, I would call it reckless indeed. Unnecessary showmanship, typical of this new breed of sailors. By the way, I heard they were a couple of Yanks."

"Hmm, that explains it."

These are the instructions I left on the boat for Madame Richardson's son:

Welcome to TAI O HAE, a sailboat with many problems. This is a list of important messages to save you a bit of time and a lot of aggravation.

1. Close aft head seacock after use. It leaks badly. Forward head does not work.

2. All valves and seacocks in the engine room are closed. The Perkins diesel and Petter Generator do not work.

3. The fuel tanks are useless and contaminated. If, for some reason, you try to start the generator, use the plastic jerry can in the cockpit, which is led to the generator lift pump. The odds of the generator starting are about 1 in 1,000,000.

4. Water tanks are foul. Use bottled water for drinking.

5. Service batteries have been charging for a while. Hopefully, you'll have enough power for the short voyage to Dieppe. They don't hold much of a charge. Try to avoid using much power.

6. Autopilot, SatNav, radar, log, speedo, RDF, and VHF do not work at this moment. Suggest you bring a handheld VHF.

7. Main compass has a 30-degree error on most easterly headings.

8. None of stove-top burners ever worked. You must cook everything in the oven.

A complete list of suggested repairs is noted in the log. Have a nice trip and give my best to your mother.

Sincerely,
John Kretschmer

*   *   *

"It always seems like it's night time on a boat," Lesa remarked. "But as long as there is a full moon and the water is full of phosphorescence, I don't mind, even if we still have the reverse tradewinds. I am glad to hear that you finally did the right thing with that damned pilot chart. By the way, when do you think we will arrive at Grand Turk?"

"We should make landfall around first light."

"Does that mean we'll be up most of the night?"

"Probably."

"I am having a hard time complaining after listening to your stories, but you never let on before we left that deliveries are so much work, so tiring."

"Work, this is an easy one, so far."

"Was the TAI O HAE really that bad or were you embellishing the story on my account?"

"No, actually, there were even more problems than I told you about, but I'm afraid if I give you the full story, you'll abandon me in Grand Turk."

Lesa smiled and nodded her head. "That's a good point. If you don't tell me about a few nice boats and nice trips soon, there is a very real possibility that I might skip ship. Now, back to our studies. A sloop has one mast, a ketch has two with the front one bigger than the back one, and a schooner, hey wait a minute, wasn't TAI O HAE a schooner?"

"Ya, why?"

"Then I don't want to know how many masts a schooner has."

◁▷

CHAPTER 9

Force
Unlucky

In human affairs there is no snug harbor, no rest short of the grave. We are forever setting forth afresh across new and stormy seas.

SAMUEL ELIOT MORISON, The European Discovery of America

I AM NOT SURE whether it was strategic career planning, mere coincidence or a subconscious stab at survival but after the TAI O HAE voyage, I began to deliver better boats. And it is a good thing too, because, as if to challenge me for sailing Swans, Hinckleys, Oysters, Oceans and Hylas, cunning Neptune threw dirty weather my way whenever possible. From an instantly legendary Cape Hatteras snorter, to Hurricanes Grace and Bob, to a Force too-much-blow in the wintry North Atlantic, it seemed as if I encountered storm conditions every time I put to sea.

The Cape Hatteras lighthouse at the eastern elbow of North Carolina's capricious Outer Banks has guided mariners around deadly Diamond Shoals for more than 100 years. From the shadow of the black and white spire I gazed out at gray seas. I thought of the 600 wrecks that litter the banks like old pickup trucks in a Kentucky yard and gave a silent salute to the many sailors resting in watery graves. I felt an eerie chill on my spine and heard my grandmother's gravelly voice for the first time in years, "But for the grace of God, there go I." Fortunately, my morbid reverie was interrupted when a nearby older lady, her hair in curlers, howled with joy as she reeled a sizable blowfish up the beach.

I struck a conversation with the fisherwoman and her husband but they seemed suspicious when I told them that I was delivering a boat from New York to Fort Lauderdale and had just stopped off to write a story about the Cape Hatteras lighthouse. "Really, it's not all than unusual." I explained defensively, "I deliver sailboats for a living." After I convinced them that I wasn't a drug smuggler and, more importantly, that I wasn't from New York, the old man became curious about my voyage.

"You stay in the waterway, don't you, son?"

"Not usually, it's a lot faster to sail on the outside."

"Hmm," the old man was thinking. Glancing at me sideways like an iguana, he offered some advice. "Well, son, I don't mean to tell no man his business, but I lived my whole life out here and I don't like the look of them clouds. This bein' October and all, and this bein' the banks, if I was you, son, I don't think I'd be sailin' nowheres too far in the necks for a couple of days."

I nodded politely and assured him I'd be careful, but the truth is I don't like anyone telling me my business. I had plenty of material for my article and was anxious to get on with the delivery. I have never easily mixed deliveries and cruising. When I am taking a boat from A to B I am focused on my task and resent any delays, even magazine assignments. After a voyage is done, I'm content to linger. My friend Dave and I hopped in the rent-a-car and hurried back to the marina at Morehead City.

We were delivering an older but well-maintained Swan 41 on the southbound leg of her annual migration between Fort Lauderdale and New York. I had met Dave McGowan years before in Sri Lanka and we reconnected when he sailed into Fort Lauderdale to complete a circumnavigation with his father. Bobby Truett, who was part of the Carolina crew of HERE AND NOW, also joined us in New York. The three of us rode a cold front south, completing the 400-mile passage around Cape Hatteras to Morehead City, North Carolina, in just over two days. Bobby left the boat there and was replaced by Nancy, who had attended one of my lectures and was anxious for bluewater experience.

We cleared Beaufort Inlet at dusk and sailed on a close reach toward the spot where the watery sun disappeared into a cold, ill-defined horizon. A carmine sky introduced the dawn and the VHF forecast called for near-gale conditions, 30 to 35 knots from the west with seas to 10 feet. Dave and I were not overly concerned. We had a lot of confidence in the boat and in ourselves and we even had the gall to call the forecast a blessing in disguise. "If we can stay out of the Gulf Stream, we might make Lauderdale in three days," I boasted. "That's only 200 miles a day and this boat loves to go upwind."

The spider legs of Frying Pan Shoals light tower were still visible when the winds began to pipe up. In a matter of hours, a strong southwest wind emerged and forced us to tack offshore, right into the teeth of the Gulf Stream current. The forecast continued to call for west and even northwest winds. Ever sanguine, Dave and I imagined a screaming close reach, riding the counter current just inside the edge of the Gulf Stream, when the winds clocked around. Unfortunately, the weather was not listening to the radio. Soon, hungry clouds intent on gobbling up the remaining specs of blue sky cast a dreary hue upon the water. My brain reluctantly resigned itself to what my senses already knew: We were in for a blow, a real blow.

By nightfall, the southwest winds topped 40 knots consistently and the barometer was free falling. Typical of many boats that I deliver but atypical of most Swans, we had only one headsail, a 150 percent roller-furled jenny. We rolled in as much headsail as we dared and tied in the second reef in the main. Nancy was miserable and useless. She settled into the one dry bunk below and we didn't see her for a couple of days. Dave and I stood two-hour watches. Without an autopilot, we were prisoners of the helm and without a spray dodger, we came to know many waves personally. By the end of my first watch, the wind was routinely pegging the meter at 54 knots.

Down below the shrieking sounded like something conjured up by Steven Spielberg. Dave, however, was having the time of his life and I could hear him shouting and singing amid the din of an angry ocean. Around midnight I wrestled the mainsail down. The wind had finally come around and we reached south under furled headsail alone. Huge confused seas continued to sweep over the boat, dousing us as we stood prone but securely harnessed to the binnacle. Dave and I had reached a strange and wonderful destination: We were in harmony with the sea and with our boat. We exuberantly accepted Neptune's fury. It was a beautiful spectacle to behold.

The storm persisted into the next morning and the seas, the result of colliding winds and currents, had become mountainous.

But our nimble Sparkman and Stephens-designed Swan skidded down steep waves with the surefootedness of a puma on a rocky ledge. The boat never gave us an anxious moment. Around noon, the front passed and the storm began to abate as quickly as it had formed. The next morning, somewhere off the Georgia coast, we were gliding along in flat seas and light airs. Later that day, we heard on the radio that the storm had baffled forecasters and laced the Outer Banks with steady winds of 80 knots and gusts to 100. A few bridges were knocked out and a barge was sunk in one of the deadliest unpredicted storms in years. It seems the old man on the beach knew his business, and the violent history of the Outer Banks continues to be written.

Back in Fort Lauderdale, I was as busy as I wanted to be delivering boats and writing sailing and travel articles. It was at this time that I met Dick Jachney, the founder and president of Caribbean Yacht Charters. His company, which is based in Marblehead, Massachusetts, has offered bareboat charters in the Virgin Islands for 25 years. Through the process of upgrading the quality of his fleet, Dick has become the primary importer of Hylas sailboats. Built by Queen Long, in Taiwan, the Hylas line has evolved from stout, good-sailing charter boats to stout, good-sailing, world-class yachts. Dick and I became friends and I quickly became CYC's number one delivery captain.

Each new Hylas is shipped from the factory to Miami and then ferried to a yard in Fort Lauderdale for commissioning. It was my task to take the boats straight from the yard to the charter base in St. Thomas, a mere 1,000-mile, dead-to-weather sea trial. To make matters more interesting, Dick usually rounded up the crew, which invariably consisted of the new and excited, but woefully inexperienced owners, and other promising prospects. Their qualifications for crew were based more on their personal income statements than sailing résumés. I delivered a slew of new Hylas 44s and 47s south. Ironically, I came to enjoy the diversity of the crew as much as the passage. Although we usually were treading completely different life paths, we had mutual respect and I made many lasting friendships. Dick's charter program afforded people the opportunity to have a beautiful boat in the Caribbean without the commitment of day-to-day ownership. From Jerry and Phyllis, a retired couple living in the desert of New Mexico, to Paul and Peggy, who

The crew of SOUTHERN LIGHT, a Hylas 44 sloop, before the CYC offshore navigation program and their encounter with Hurricane Bob.

had a rags to riches story to tell, to Scott, Jim and Skip, entrepreneurs who dreamed of sailing off into the sunset but realized that they weren't quite ready, I was always intrigued by the people who chose to buy into the charter program.

Tony Seibert, who builds luxury condos in Vail, Colorado, was a frequent crew on my deliveries. Tony owned a Hylas 47 and while he loved the way the boat performed, there were many design features, especially from the standpoint of comfort, that he knew he could improve upon. Tony always sailed with a tape measure and made copious notes of what worked and what didn't. He and Dick had decided to update the 47 and although Sparkman and Stephens would be credited with the design, Tony did most of the development. From riding the long, slashing breakers left over from Hurricane Grace to meandering over Gulf Stream swells and through Gulf Stream squalls, Tony logged thousands of miles accompanying me on deliveries to St. Thomas, Annapolis and Newport. The result of his research and Dick's requirements was the Hylas 49, which soon became the queen of the CYC fleet. The 49 also sold in record numbers to sailors who had no interest in chartering and forced the sailing community to take notice of Hylas as something more than just nice charter boats.

My successful deliveries with disparate crews convinced Dick that we could make money while ferrying the boats from the Caribbean to the Northeast for the annual fall boat shows. The CYC Offshore Delivery and Navigation course sold out promptly as we discovered that there were many people craving an opportunity to sail offshore. I was the director of the program and we scheduled two boats and four legs: St. Thomas to Nassau; Nassau to Newport, Rhode Island; and then returning after the shows: Annapolis to Nassau, Nassau to St. Thomas. Leg one provided the sea stories.

I skippered a Hylas 44 SOUTHERN LIGHT and my mate was Max, son of my friend Edd Kalehoff and just 16. Max is a fine sailor and he should be; he made his first Bermuda passage when he was nine months old and had lived aboard his dad's classic yawl MAGIC VENTURE most of his life. We were joined by four paying crew members: Harold, a hulking Washington bureaucrat; Tim, a San Francisco dentist longing for adventure; Ben, a fast-track executive who needed some time away; and Roger, a retired engineer who had always dreamed of making an offshore passage. We spent a day in St. Thomas and I gave the crews of both boats an intensive primer in celestial navigation. Although it was the heart of hurricane season, the tropical weather outlook looked clear when we set off on August 5.

The first order of business, emergency procedures for abandoning ship and retrieving a man overboard, had a sobering effect on the crew. I never make hard and fast rules on a boat. Rules don't mix well in my recipe for life and I feel that ultimately everybody is responsible for their own safety as well as everything else in their

lives. I did, however, strongly suggest that they wear a safety harness at night and when working on deck, especially when I was
below. I had stashed a coconut aboard to emphasize my point. I
told the crew to watch me throw the coconut overboard and then
had them close their eyes for two minutes. Nobody, myself included, could spot the coconut, which is about the size of a human
head, after the interval. The conditions were typical of the
tradewinds, 15 to 20 knots of breeze and rolling, six-foot seas.

The close confines of a small boat either breed camaraderie or
conflict. Luckily, all aboard sensed the deep spiritual meaning of
our enterprise. Joseph Conrad noted, "All things can be found at
sea, according to the spirit of the quest." We each had our own private quests. Ben, the businessman, was searching for the perfect
limerick to describe our mortal enemy, the crew of the other boat.
Harold, who lumbered across the deck like a runaway Mack truck,
was so cheerful that it didn't matter that he gybed within seconds
anytime he took the helm. Roger, the engineer, was hoping that at
least one of his celestial sights would place us in the Northern
Hemisphere. Tim was surprised how well we were all getting along
and also at how much he enjoyed being at sea. "I never expected
that this passage would actually be fun," he said with a laugh. Max,
a devoted fisherman, tended his Cuban hand line with diligence
but no luck. I longed to sleep four consecutive hours without hearing the words, "Sorry to bother you skipper, but . . ."

The irony of hurricane season in the tropics is that if nothing
ugly and circular is brewing in the atmosphere, the sailing conditions are usually quite good. Glorious days of tradewind sailing
whisked us toward our first landfall, San Salvador, a Bahamian out
island. A routine was established and the crew took to sharing all
shipboard activities with gusto. We even dropped sail and took a
brief swim as we passed over the Puerto Rican Trench, which, at
30,000 feet, is the deepest spot in the Atlantic. On the one hand,
the crew felt like they were already salty veterans of the sea, ready
for anything old Neptune could throw at them. On the other hand,
however, and I'm sure they will all deny this, their shoreside worlds
were never far away. Before the end of day two, pictures of wives,
children and grandchildren were being circulated about the cockpit.

To my surprise, they were serious about celestial navigation
and I worked hard showing them the tricks of the trade. A day

from San Salvador, I turned over all navigational responsibilities to the crew. Anticipating an early-morning arrival, they took an astonishing array of sextant sights. Working primarily with the sun, which is the most reliable target for celestial navigators, they carefully reduced their sights and plotted the results. A consensus position was tough to find; their combined plots looked like a child's creation on an Etch-a-Sketch. Star sights provide a more accurate fix, and don't require accurate dead reckoning between sights. But a shaky round of twilight star sights did little to quell the mounting anxiety of impending landfall. The supposedly powerful light on the eastern shore of the island was out, not an uncommon occurrence in the Bahamas, and the crew accused me of convincing the Bahamian officials to shut off the light just for our voyage. The tension built all night. At first light, San Salvador loomed dead ahead, about 10 miles away, just as predicted and pandemonium ensued. I couldn't help but think the whooping and hollering of my crew must have rivaled the celebration of Columbus's crew 499 years before.

We moored the boats at Riding Rock Marina, near the small settlement of Cockburn Town. San Salvador was called Watling's Island before a far-sighted official snatched the name away from nearby Cat Island in 1926. A scrubby, overgrown coral reef, San Salvador is the island that may have been Columbus' first landfall in the New World. The quiet, sparsely-populated island was reluctantly preparing for a big bash, the 500th anniversary celebration of Columbus' voyage. Club Med was building a resort and new statues of dashing Cristoforo were springing up around the island. We visited the New World Museum, housed in the former jail, which hadn't been used in five years. The museum contained an eclectic assortment of old bottles, some movie posters and black and white photos of salt mines. The beauty of the New World Museum was that it had nothing to do with the discovery of the New World.

We wanted to be away before darkness and hitched a ride back to the marina. The driver was not pleased about the big plans the government in Nassau had for the island. "A minister came out here a while back. He was full of promises. He said there is going to be a big party. Well, I don't want it. We don't need it. I don't want the Queen of England to come to our little island," he told us. "Maybe Princess Di, but not that stuffy old lady. What's she going to do here anyway, dedicate another statue? They should just leave us alone. They're complicating everything. They even say that there'll be so many cars on the island that we'll need three digits for our license plates."

Before sunset San Salvador disappeared astern and we were charging toward Nassau with much at stake, the last boat in had to buy dinner. The next morning we were greeted by a red sky and Tim asked, "Is there any truth to that old saying, red sky by morning, sailors take warning?"

"Sometimes," I said casually. I knew however, from the building clouds and falling barometer that some weather was moving our way. I didn't know that before the day was out we would be battling a rapidly moving hurricane.

The weather thickened as the wind backed from the east to the northwest, a sure sign of developing low pressure. Soon it was blowing a gale and we were forced to beat into choppy seas. I told the crew to take some time to carefully stow their belongings below and to break out the foulweather gear. We had no weather forecasting equipment aboard except the barometer; however, a radio chat with a passing freighter informed us that we were right smack in the middle of the projected path of a tropical storm that had just been named Bob. Once again, a male storm was poised to make my life miserable. Bob sounded worse than Floyd. Bob is a nice name but so prosaic. Imagine loosing your boat in Tropical Storm Bob. It just doesn't sound very romantic. The hurricane center could have at least called the storm Robert.

Trying to put a positive spin on our sudden change of fortunes, I told the crew that, as long as you're in a good boat with a good crew, a storm at sea is an interesting and enlightening experience. "You not only must confront your fears, but also take an active part in assuring your survival," I said cheerfully. I should have used a different word. Before my silly little speech, nobody had even considered that they would not survive. A serious mood swept over the boat, especially when we learned a few hours later that the storm had been upgraded to a hurricane.

Roger, who was the oldest aboard, took a nasty fall from the companionway steps. He was in agony and fortunately Tim, the only one with medical training, took charge of the situation. He suspected that Roger had broken a few ribs and carefully eased him into the aft bunk, supporting him as best he could. He attended to him on his off-watches and also assumed his deck duties. It is a frightening feeling—there is no other way to describe it—waiting for a hurricane to overrun you. I had ruled out trying to seek shelter. There were no secure harbors within reach, and I firmly believe that a well-handled boat at sea, with sufficient sea room, is safer than one in a jam-packed harbor. We were approximately 50 miles north of San Salvador and 40 miles east of Cat Island, with infinite room to run north and east, when we felt the first of Bob's outer storm bands.

Once again the only headsail aboard was a roller-furling genoa and, as the winds strengthened, we rolled it in until it was about the size of a hand towel, just enough sail area to provide some steering control. I told Max, Tim and Harold that we had to check the furling line frequently for signs of chafe. "If the line chafes through and the sail unfurls, it will be a disaster." The main was lashed to the boom and the bimini was lashed to the deck. "This seems surreal," Tim said, as we were pelted by blistering winds and stinging rain.

"What's surreal about it?" I said, shouting to be heard over the shrieking storm. "I'm holding on for dear life on my first passage in a hurricane. But instead of being afraid, I feel alive, I feel free." I smiled, Tim understood. What made the scene even harder to comprehend was the sight of big Harold at the helm. He was just happy that he couldn't gybe the mainsail and he shook his head like a wet dog each time a wave crashed over the boat.

"My wife had some vague notion that this was a luxury cruise," he said, chortling. "If she could see me now. You should have seen the look on her face when I told her I was going to learn to use a sextant," he added just as a freight train of a wave completely soaked him. "Oh boy, that was a good run!" Then he broke into a chorus of "Roll me over in the clover." It was going to take more than a hurricane to ruin Harold's day.

The only good thing about Bob was that he was in a hurry. He was moving at more than 20 miles per hour and having formed only a few hundred miles away from our position, there wasn't time for him to whip the seas to dangerous heights. Bob did, however, pass directly over us and for the second time in my life I experienced the eerie calm in the eye of the storm. By the time of Bob's final act when the southern edge of the tightly packed low-pressure system passed over us, we were already making plans to get back on course for Nassau. I couldn't reach the other boat on the VHF but I was sure they had ridden out the storm as ably as we had. Twelve hours later we were becalmed, rolling miserably on dying soldiers, leftover swells. We eased Roger back into the cockpit, broke out the San Salvador rum and the war stories began in earnest. I had to chuckle; less than a day after the fury had subsided, the winds and waves were already growing stronger and larger. I could just imagine what the conditions would be like by the time the crew described the encounter with Bob to friends and colleagues back home. But I never begrudge sea stories, especially when they are well-earned.

In between my Hylas ramblings there were many deliveries. I took a Hinckley Bermuda 40 from St. Thomas up to Buzzards Bay. I came to know the Sullivan brothers, Paul and Dan. Paul was the owner and Dan the older brother. We laughed our way up the ocean. I ran a Gulfstar 60 across the pond to Marbella, Spain, where I picked up an Oyster 39 and beat against the Portuguese trades back to England. I took a Spindrift 43 with a ramshackle crew through the Canal to Costa Rica. Without question, however, the most demanding and probably most dangerous voyage I have ever undertaken was the delivery of CIGON/ISOBELL. She was a 20-year-old Ocean 71 and I agreed to take her from Newport, Rhode Island, to Stockholm, Sweden—in January!

Of course, the logical question is: Why would anybody deliver a boat to Sweden in the middle of the winter? Why not wait a few months for moderate spring weather? The answers are economic, personal and, of course, illogical. The owners, two young Swedes, Max and Martin, wanted the boat in Stockholm as soon as possible and as a delivery skipper, you generally do what the owners desire if you want to be paid. A midwinter delivery to Sweden isn't cheap and nothing can make a skipper overlook a few double-digit gale percentages on a pilot chart faster than the prospect of a fat pay-check. Most importantly, after nine transatlantic deliveries, I had grown complacent with the crossing. I was stirred by the challenge of doing it at the worst possible time. Also, I confess, I was having a bit of a personal crisis. My 35th birthday was looming and despite

CIGON/ISOBELL, an Ocean 71, at the dock in Newport, awaiting her stormy crossing.

all of my delivery adventures and misadventures, I had a powerful desire to prove that I was still the same person who beat around Cape Horn the wrong way in a 32-foot boat. Sometimes the male ego defies all forms of reason.

Even I wouldn't test the wintry North Atlantic in just any boat and the Ocean 71, designed by the fine Dutch consortium of Van de Stadt and Co., and built by Southern Ocean Shipyard in England, was ideal for the crossing. Although we had the usual ration of mechanical problems that accompany any long delivery, especially when a boat has been sitting on the hard for a couple of years, the ruggedly constructed, cutter-rigged ketch easily stood up to six weeks of near-continual gale-force conditions. Also her sheer size and center-cockpit design allowed us to remain relatively dry, which is the key to happiness in severe conditions.

Finding crew for this passage required all of my charm and a bit of cunning. Most people I contacted just laughed and shook their heads; they were not even remotely interested. Good old Molly, who of all people should have known better, was coerced by a combination of pity and greed. She knew how badly I wanted to make the voyage and the money was good, too good. She agreed to sail on leg one, Newport to the Azores. I needed a capable mate for the entire voyage and this person had to be both experienced and, more importantly, able to tolerate long stretches of misery. Naturally I sought a Brit. The English seem to thrive in nasty weather and my friend Joe Murton was actually honored that I asked him to come along. Although Joe was my first choice, I didn't have the heart to tell him that he was also the only person to agree to make the whole trip.

I had met Joe and his girlfriend Vicki in the Caribbean years before and we had sailed together a few times. He was building a steel boat near London and they were planning a world cruise. He was eager to gain some heavy-weather experience and made me promise that we would encounter a few gales. That was one promise I knew I would be able to keep.

Joe joined me in Newport on January 20 and we spent four furious days preparing the boat for the crossing. The boat, which was then called CIGON but in the Azores would become ISOBELL, was lying in the Little Harbor Yacht Yard. Bobby Hood, one of Ted's sons, ran the yard and was most helpful although he was convinced we were completely crazy. Working in sub-freezing temperatures, we installed new batteries and rewired a good part of the electrical system. We serviced all 16 through-hull fittings and had to rebuild much of the plumbing system because numerous hoses had frozen and cracked during the unusually cold winter. We had an electrician repair the autopilot and Joe discovered and replaced a cracked universal joint on the steering system. We launched the boat on January 25.

As we loaded provisions aboard, the insurance company's hapless surveyor arrived for the third time in a week. The underwriters were understandably concerned about the voyage and we had complied with all of the surveyor's recommendations. Marine surveyors are not, as a breed, my favorite people. They insist on sounding like experts on all subjects, whether nautical or not, and have cowardly or brilliantly, depending how you look at it, mastered the art of covering their asses with mumbo-jumbo disclaimers in their reports. The real survey of a boat always takes place when it is delivered. Anyway, this so-called expert was ready to scuttle the voyage unless I signed off on his route recommendation. This idiot wanted me to head for the Canary Islands, a mere 2,000-mile detour in a 4,000-mile voyage. That is like driving from New York to Florida via Texas. Also he wanted me to promise not to use the sails, unless it was an emergency, and motor all the way across the pond.

I was incredulous. I tried to explain the nature of sailboats and that I planned to hover around the 40th parallel until the Azores before sailing north for the English Channel and the North Sea. Only by promising that I would keep the Canary Islands as my first option and that we would take the sails down at every chance would he sign the release form that approved the coverage.

Just before midnight on January 26, I backed CIGON out of her slip. The 2,000-mile haul to Horta was our sea trial. Joe was the one who nicknamed me Captain Pangloss and I must admit I do begin every voyage with an absurd sense of optimism. The weather was cold but gentle as we made our way east, past the George's Banks. I told Joe and Molly that if we reached the Gulf Stream without a real blow, we'd be in good shape. They were both wise enough not to believe me and two days out a series of icy rain squalls gave us a taste of what the North Atlantic held in store. The squalls began to run together and soon a westerly gale developed on the morning of February 1, a day and night I'd like to forget but probably never will.

All through the day we reduced sail and when evening watches began CIGON was under staysail alone, surfing down waves at 14 knots. Molly, who had the first watch, noted wryly, "At least the surveyor is happy, we don't have much sail up." At 2100 she poked her head below and shouted, "We've lost the staysail." Joe and I struggled into our wet gear and dashed forward. The halyard had chafed through and the staysail was dangling in the water alongside. We wrestled it aboard, lashed it to the lifelines and hauled the storm jib to the foredeck. For some reason, the luff had been altered for the headstay furling gear so we tacked the storm jib to the staysail tack pendant and hoisted it loose-luffed.

The storm jib provided enough directional stability to engage the autopilot and I dropped below to call a nearby ship whose lights were only occasionally visible in the blown spray and towering seas. According to the radio operator on the Dutch tanker TANIA JACOB, the storm winds were steady at Force 12, hurricane strength, and gusting to Force 13. "Force 13," I screamed back into the mike, "I thought the Beaufort scale only went to 12." The

Wrestling with the staysail aboard CIGON.

remarkably calm voice chuckled and replied, "Well, skipper, call it Force Unlucky."

Unfortunately, just as the boat was finding her stride, a black square wave, out of sequence from the others, crashed into CIGON amidships and we skidded off course. With a thundering shudder, the storm jib backed. The tack pendant exploded and the small jib flew upward, making a grotesque imitation of a drunken Chinese kite. After sweeping the masthead clean of various lights, antennas and wind instruments, the sail plummeted into the water and, together with the sheet, wrapped around the prop shaft for all it was worth.

Joe dashed below to check the strain on the shaft while I frantically tried to cut the halyard which had jammed in the mast.

"How bad is it, Joe?" I asked as he returned topsides. "It sounds pretty bad from up here, like it's going to tear the shaft right out of the boat."

"It sounds worse down there. John, we need to cut that sail free with some urgency," Joe said quietly but with a seriousness I had never heard before. Then he added, "I suspect the shaft is already badly bent."

With Molly steering under bare poles, Joe pulled the sail toward the boat and I cut away madly. The phosphorescence crashing aboard shed eerie light on an otherwise gloomy night. It took

Force Unlucky, in the cold, February North Atlantic.

me a moment to realize that I cut my knuckle clean off. There was
no time to worry about it. I stuck it back in place, held it with my
left forefinger and kept slashing. I managed to slice the sheet free
but the sail was still snagged. Joe wrestled as much of it alongside
as he could and leaning over the rail as far as I dared, I cut it to bits
and it finally disappeared into the black depths. As Joe and I lay
panting on the deck, for some ominous reason the spreader lights
came on and cast a spotlight on the blood-stained deck.

Before we could even catch our breath, a jarring noise sent us
flying below. I pulled open the engine room door and saw the disaster immediately. The generator, an archaic, mean-spirited, 12-
kilowatt Onan that didn't even run, had sheared its mounts and
toppled into the main diesel. I threw myself at the Onan, which was
not a small or light piece of equipment, and propped my back
against it. Somehow I forced it back upright and Joe lashed it in
place. Once we were sure that it was secure, we made our way back
to the cockpit. We couldn't help but laugh. What else could go
wrong in one evening? "I don't know or want to know," Molly
chipped in, "but I do know it's your watch, captain."

When the winds finally eased three days later we were able to
assess the damage and enact repairs. Joe hoisted me up both masts
and I secured the VHF and SSB antennas and rove a new staysail
halyard. We repaired the staysail and gradually made our floating

world shipshape. Miraculously, the shaft was still usable and the main engine didn't sustain any serious damage. A transatlantic delivery would not be complete without some kind of diesel problem. On the only calm day of the passage when it would have been nice to rumble along under power, the big Perkins developed an air lock and refused to run. Eventually we traced the problem to the lift pump, which didn't have enough umph to draw fuel up from the bilge tanks. Once again I had to design a jury-rigged day tank, but by the time I conned the engine to life, the westerlies had returned. Indeed, we rode a hard, 40-knot southwest gale into Horta, 14 days out from Newport.

With Joe Murton, using delicate tools to repair the staysail in the main saloon of CIGON.

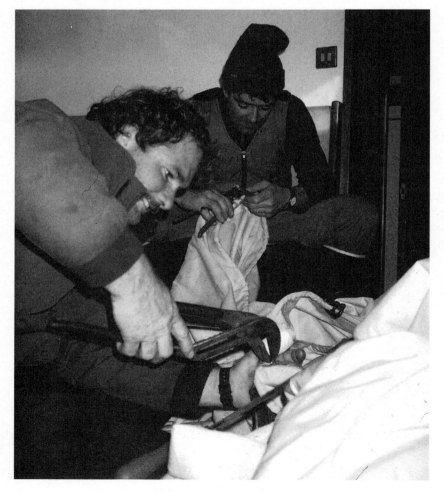

We had the dubious distinction of being the first yacht to call at Horta that year and my friend José Azevedo was convinced that I had finally lost my mind. José, who had taken over the day-to-day operations of Café Sport, just shook his bearded head. "It's February, captain, February. Why are you always in such a hurry? Just stay here with us for a few months." At that moment, with another cold Atlantic blowing just outside the door, José's offer was tempting. But, well, you know the routine by now. Needless to say we pressed on.

Molly left the boat in Horta, both literally and figuratively. We had sailed together for the last time. When I returned from Sweden a couple months later, she had gone her own way. Steve Maseda, a friend from Los Angeles, joined us for the next leg, a 1,300-mile passage to Plymouth, England. A lawyer in real life, Steve had just finished a year-long sabbatical with his family aboard their Gulfstar 50 sloop in the Caribbean. He was having trouble readjusting to land life and, to the dismay of his partners not to mention his wife, he accepted my offer to crew. The fact that Steve would rather test his mettle in the February gales that rake the Bay of Biscay instead of working, made me realize that there must be something to all those lawyer jokes. From Horta onwards, the boat was called ISOBELL, as the official Swedish registration had come through.

No sooner had Graciosa, the northernmost island in the Archipelago, dipped beneath the horizon, than the wind began to howl again. On the night of February 17, I recorded a typical log entry: "2300, tough night. All hands up to reef main at 2100 after wild gybe and boat rounding up. It is cold, damned cold and blowing at least 8, with gusts to 9, maybe even 10. It's just blowing. But we're doing fine with the staysail and three reefs, screaming toward merry old England. Joe made spaghetti for dinner."

It took several days to shake stubborn easterlies before the westerly gales returned and whisked us north. The SatNav never worked and GPS, in the early 90s, was still very expensive and only for sailors who didn't know how to navigate anyway. I relied on my trusty old Freiberger sextant for the approach to the English Channel. I was nervous, the leaden sky had not given me a glimpse of the sun for several days and ISOBELL was flying, at times hitting 16 knots as we surfed down the face of huge waves. The truth is as

Joe Murton and Steve Maseda, working the foredeck in typical conditions.

land and rock drew ever closer, I would have given my left thumb, the one with cobbled up knuckle, for a GPS. While I was fretting about my very uncertain dead-reckoning position and Steve was concentrating on steering, Joe was in a world of his own.

Once again, I witnessed that bizarre and beautiful state when a person finds complete harmony in a gale, when nature's fury seems natural, not terrifying. Nearing the coast of the mother country, Joe was euphoric. Although the wind was laced with snow and the decks were often awash, Joe spent hours on the bow and at the helm hooting, hollering and even singing, something he admitted that he does not do often. "I can't actually remember ever singing before," he told me later when I teased him about his spirited version of Rod Stewart's 'Maggie'.

"Really, John, you of all people should not offer critiques of someone else's singing." Luckily, aptly named Lizard Point loomed out of the low scud just where I thought it should.

Steve, a stalwart crew but with a new fondness for the law, left the boat in Plymouth and Joe's girlfriend Vicki joined us for what we hoped might be a pleasurable 24-hour sail down the Channel to the Solent. What were we thinking? Pleasurable and English Channel are words that should never be used in the same sentence, not even the same paragraph. Forty-eight hours later, we worked our way into Portsmouth Harbour through the thickest fog I have

Joe Murton, at the helm, driving ISOBELL in a full gale approaching England.

ever sailed in. Vicki's short holiday had become the most stressful leg of the voyage. Without radar, we might still be drifting about the channel.

Joe and I began to smell the finish line. On February 27 we set off across the North Sea. Short, square brown waves seemed to hit ISOBELL from every direction, at times bringing 50 tons of fiberglass to a shuddering stop. At least the navigation was easy. The numerous oil rigs are well charted and arranged in groups. We lurched from rig to rig, checking them off the chart like items on a grocery list. Three days out of Portsmouth we entered the Kiel estuary. We tried to sail against the ebbing Elbe River but after netting just five miles in three hours, decided to anchor and wait for slack water.

The Kiel Canal, a 60-mile ditch with a couple of locks, slices across the Danish/German Peninsula, providing a short-cut into the Baltic Sea. Around midnight we arrived at Brunsbüttel, the western terminus of the canal. I suspected that there would be paperwork to complete and that we would transit the canal the following morning. I radioed the lock master to request permission to tie up for the night. A stern, but obviously female voice, came cackling back at me, "Prepare to enter the small boat lock 9 chamber, immediately."

Surprised, I asked, "Is the canal open at this hour?"

Now the voice was irritated. In precise but clipped English it replied, "Captain, this is Germany. Make a note that the Kiel Canal is open 24 hours a day, every day of the year. Please enter the lock chamber immediately."

Although the northern light was slow to arrive, we had plenty of time to enjoy the rolling pastureland that borders what was formerly called the Kaiser Wilhelm Canal. The earth-tone shades of gentle land looking hopefully toward spring were refreshing and in sharp contrast to weeks of angry blue horizons. Sadly, I bid Joe farewell in Kiel. Our friendship had been tested and forged by North Atlantic gales. We both had a powerful feeling that we had accomplished an impressive task but typically we left things unsaid. As he boarded the train, Joe laughed and said, "Well, John, I must say you kept your promise about the gales, thanks."

ISOBELL's new owners Max and Martin joined me in Kiel for the final 500-mile sail to Stockholm. The Baltic blessed us with fair winds and clear skies. After a brief stop on the lovely Danish island of Lolland, we charged north under spinnaker. Max and Martin were like kids on Christmas morning; they wanted to play with all their new toys. They laughed at me when I suggested that we motor in light airs. Instead, we trimmed the spinnaker vigorously and hoisted the mizzen staysail to keep ISOBELL moving. We skirted the island of Bornholm and then hugged the Swedish shoreline, passing inside of the slender island of Öland. Max was determined to show me something of the coast and we detoured into the medieval harbor of Kalmar. The only event to mar our three-day passage from Kiel was a sudden fire in the engine room. The starter motor became mysteriously engaged and began to burn. I smelled the fire and by the time I reached the engine room there were a few lively flames dancing about. I drained a nearby extinguisher, which quickly snuffed out the fire. Fortunately, other than a few charred wires, there wasn't serious damage and we had a spare starter that I promptly installed. The worst job was cleaning up the dry chemical residue.

We skirted Visby on the island of Gotland before entering the Skargarden, an archipelago of 20,000 islands and a maze of waterways leading to Stockholm. We had the islands to ourselves in early March and a light easterly wind was perfect for negotiating narrow channels under sail. More than once our intended route to the capital was blocked by ice, and one time we were beset and had to hack our way back to open waters using the boat hook and dinghy paddles. Just before sunset on March 6 with gilded spires of the magnificent stone buildings that line Stockholm's inner harbor aglow with red light, I eased ISOBELL into her slip on Skeppsholmen Island. As I secured the mooring lines, I instructed a bizarre sculptured zebra wearing a black rubber tie (the museum of modern art overlooked the harbor) to keep an eye on the old girl.

*   *   *

We were sitting on a crooked bench in a plywood shack overlooking a fringing reef that offers minimal protection for Grand Turk's roadstead of a harbor. We were munching mouth-scorching conch fritters, or as the wrinkled old lady who made them called them, "hot rhythm pills." The man sitting next to us had clothespins stuck to his face.

It was good to be off SIREN'S SONG, if only for an afternoon. Lesa looked like she belonged on the sun-bleached island that stands apart from the other islands in the Turks and Caicos group. She is a tropical girl. But tropical or not, she never cuts you any slack.

"So, captain, surviving three monumental storms is your idea of a nice story?"

"Well, not really nice, but you wanted to hear about good boats and those were good boats."

"But you got the shit knocked out of you. Is that fun?"

I squirmed on the bench and snagged my shorts on a protruding nail. Finally I mumbled, "In a way, yes, I mean, to know that you can endure and press on."

Lesa scrunched her face in an exaggerated way and looking at me quizzically said, "You have a strange idea of fun."

"I'm not saying storms are fun, that is not my point. But during a storm, you feel so alive, every second is valuable, and sometimes unbelievably long. If we lived our lives in storm conditions, they would seem 10 times longer than they really are. I love that feeling of knowing I am alive, not just existing, not just stumbling through another day and sometimes it takes a really pissed-off ocean to find that feeling."

Lesa took my left hand and examined it.

"What are you looking at?"

"Your knuckle, it grew back?"

"Ya, it sure did, but the thumb's not much good these days."

"A small price you pay for being so alive?"

"I guess so."

CHAPTER 10

A Home Delivery

They sailed away for a year and a day to the land where the bong tree grows.

EDWARD LEAR, The Owl and the Pussycat

"HOW WOULD YOU like to buy a steel boat?" Joe asked. Lesa and I were in his office to collect the balance due on the SIREN'S SONG delivery.

"Joe, I don't have any interest in buying a steel boat. You know me, I don't have a lot of money and even if I did, I wouldn't spend it on a boat. I know better."

"You don't need much money. This is a special deal. The boat is going to go cheap, real cheap."

"Joe, you're starting to sound like a yacht broker," I chided him before Lesa interrupted.

"How cheap?" she asked, surprising me with her curiosity. Sensing her interest, he grinned and said, "I'm not going to tell you until you go take a look at it."

LONE STAR, one of many boats docked behind private homes on the canals of Fort Lauderdale, was a Roberts 44 ketch. Although obviously homebuilt, she had nice lines despite hard chines. Lesa was intrigued; she called it funky. But I could tell she liked the rust-streaked old girl. That Lesa could actually admire a boat like this and see that, beyond cosmetic flaws, it had great potential as a bluewater cruiser, reminded me again how fortunate I was to have stumbled across her in Belize. Even a dank, foul-smelling interior, featuring a holding tank that hadn't been emptied in years, and moldy, orange vinyl cushions couldn't dim her enthusiasm. I knew that steel boats rusted from the inside out. Any serious corrosion will show up in the bilge first and I plugged my nose and probed about. The boat was just 10 years old and the metal appeared to be in good condition.

On the way back to Joe's office as Lesa excitedly discussed her ideas for modifying the interior, I confessed my true feelings about steel boats. I had longed for a steel boat for years, ever since I first read Bernard Moitessier's enchanting books and had made a promise to myself that my next boat would be metal, like his JOSHUA. I wanted a boat that could carry me up the Orinoco to where the Yanomami lived, or down to Shackleton's South Georgia and the Antarctic, and through minefield reefs of Pacific islands far from the yellow brick road. I also wanted a boat that I couldn't break; steel suited my gentle touch. Having sailed many fine yachts, I had concluded that I wanted a funkier, less pretentious boat. I wanted more of a working boat that would be at home in rough-edged commercial harbors as well as yacht marinas.

"I've been sketching steel boats in my journals for a long time," I told Lesa.

"Then why did you tell Joe you had no interest?"

"Just to keep him on his toes. He knows I want a steel boat."

Joe explained the situation. The unfortunate Texan who owned the boat needed to sell it promptly, as in that day, and was willing to let it go for a great price. Lesa and I looked at each other and then retreated to the parking lot. We could just afford to buy the boat if we pooled our savings. Everything in our brief life together seemed to happen fast, too fast, and now we were faced with a huge decision. I was ready to walk away from the deal not because I didn't want the boat. I did. I just didn't know if I wanted the commitment. Lesa helped me see the boat in a different light.

"John," Lesa said, in a serious tone of voice I hadn't heard before, "I'm no expert about boats, we both know that, but . . . is this boat capable of sailing around the world? Can it do all the things we've talked about?"

"Not in its present condition, baby. It needs a bit of work but once that is done, the answer is yes, definitely yes."

"When you look at the way the cabins are laid out, it's perfect for a family. Don't you think so?"

"Ya."

"Do you think we can fix it up to the point that we can charter it and make a little money with it? We've been talking about an adventure charter business. This seems almost too good to be true. We aren't completely deceiving ourselves, are we?"

"I don't know. My instincts tell me that it is good boat."

"Should we buy it?"

"I don't know, Lesa. I want to haul it out, sound the bottom, and look over the whole boat real closely."

Lesa kissed me. "Let's go for it, baby, subject to survey of course. But let's go for it. Let's buy the funky boat."

"Are you sure?"

Lesa nodded, "I'm sure."

We bought the boat, paid several months dockage and then flew back to Isla Mujeres and TALISMAN. Christer had asked me to sail his boat south to the Rio Dulce in Guatemala before the summer hurricane season. Lesa and I planned to take a couple of months gunkholing our way along the coasts of Mexico and Belize. To help with expenses, I arranged a charter while in Belize. It seemed natural to be back aboard, and we fell in love all over again. We day-sailed south, stopping at Cozumel and Tulum, where we anchored in the shadow of an ancient Mayan fortress. The following night we tucked in behind the thundering reef and dropped the hook in Bahia de la Ascensión. We purchased a couple of lobsters from local fishermen and mixed up a pitcher of rum punch. We had been trying to come up with a name for our new boat because, bad luck or not, LONE STAR had to go. I've never really liked Texas or, with several exceptions, Texans, and Lesa had never even set foot in the state. Lesa liked the name FORTUNA, Spanish for luck, chance and fortune and she said, "It counters the bad luck taboo about changing names." I liked it too. I knew that it was my good fortune to have discovered Lesa and she led me to the boat, so FORTUNA it was.

After 10 days we were ready to be rid of our charter guests, two couples from suburban Chicago. Chartering is demanding work, especially when you just want to be alone, and we were both relieved as they boarded the prop plane in San Pedro, Belize. We were back where our affair had begun months before and filled with strange emotions. Lesa knew something was different inside of her, her first clue being that she had no taste for alcohol. She thought she was pregnant and I remembered that cool night in the mountains of Hispaniola—somehow you just know these things. There was no

Lesa, with lobsters for dinner in Bahia de la Ascensión, in Mexico.

such thing as a home pregnancy test in San Pedro so we made our way to the simple, wooden-framed Lion's Clinic, just past the landing strip.

The heavy-displacement nurse anchored behind the counter brusquely asked, "Whataya need?" Lesa quietly told her. She gave Lesa a small cup and in a clear, booming voice said, "Take this back there, urinate in it and bring it back up here." All eyes in the clinic followed Lesa as she walked to the bathroom. All eyes followed her as she rejoined me at the counter. The nurse dabbed the plastic

FORTUNA, a Roberts 44 ketch, purchased with Lesa.

pregnancy test and we stood holding hands, waiting. Tears welled in Lesa's eyes. Soon a little pink dot and the plus symbol emerged.

The nurse smiled, lowered her voice and said, "Miss, it's positive." My knees felt weak. Lesa squeezed my hand but calmly replied, "How much do I owe you?"

"Fifteen dollars," the nurse replied.

Lesa counted out the money and said, "Thanks, I think."

Outside, Lesa's eyes were filled with tears but her face was smiling. "I guess I can't decide whether to laugh or cry."

I hugged her until she gasped and then hugged her again.

Eventually, we left TALISMAN at Susanna's Marina at the head of the Rio Dulce, beyond the reach of the most devious hurricanes. Lesa donated most of the gear in her five boxes to the boat and we made our way back to Fort Lauderdale. Suddenly it was June, the baby was due in mid-October, Lesa and I were married, and something weird was happening to her stomach. We were aboard HO ALOHA, bound for Bermuda, the first stop on another transatlantic delivery. Lesa was determined to make the crossing and the fact that she was in her fifth month of pregnancy was not going to stop her. She was feeling great and we both dreaded the prospect of a month's separation if I made the trip alone. Besides, it is never too early for a baby to find its sea legs and I wondered if the crossing would count toward sea duty when the baby applied for her captain's license.

HO ALOHA, a Gallart 44 motorsailer, was a high-quality boat built in Spain. She was Euro-styled on deck with a modern underbody and twin 4-cylinder Volvo diesels, capable of sailing or motoring at 10 knots. The boat was designed to hurry between glitzy Mediterranean harbors, not for crossing the Atlantic. It was a boat to be seen aboard, not to actually be aboard. There was no cockpit to speak of, just a narrow foot well for the helmsman. There was, however, a huge and essentially useless sunning deck astern. The interior was done in leather and vinyl and there wasn't a single piece of exposed wood and precious few handholds to detract from the plush, motoryacht look. I knew the boat and her Dutch owner Rolf well, having sailed with him and his wife across the Gulf of Mexico the year before.

There is something about men and their boats. The sloppiest, messiest, most disorganized men ashore will frequently turn anal-retentive as soon as they set foot on their boats. They dash around with paper towels, attacking drip rings and act like you've insulted their daughter if you climb aboard with shoes on. They are more concerned about the varnish than the stock market. It is as if some latent housekeeping urge springs to life with the motion of the sea. Rolf, a witty, urbane, fun-loving guy ashore, became a bundle of highly organized nervous energy once we cast off. I confess Rolf's antics disturbed Lesa and the rest of the Dutch crew more than me. I have a wonderful ability not to take things personally. Besides, I was sleepwalking through the passage; my mind was preoccupied with my lovely wife and what was inside her ever-expanding belly.

I had assured Lesa that June was the ideal month for the crossing and the pleasant leg to Bermuda was auspicious; it was time for a nice passage. After the requisite moped ramblings around the green, rolling hills of Bermuda, which despite recent developments still seems like an island plucked from the pages of a fairy tale, we set sail for the Azores brimming with confidence. So much for June crossings. During the next 18 days and 20 hours, the Atlantic thoroughly tested the resolve of HO ALOHA's crew. We endured 9 days of full gales, including a Force 11 storm from the east that persisted for three of the longest days ever. Instead of frolicking on the sun deck, we were wrapped in foulweather gear, huddled under the fixed windscreen, cold, wet and miserable. Rolf, frustrated that he couldn't control the weather and that his boat was a mess, took it the hardest.

Twice I had to dive overboard to free propeller wraps. The generator, which was required to keep the many AC appliances, including the stove and fridge, working, was a constant source of irritation and Rolf and I spent hours in the engine room. Naturally the autopilot failed, which meant long tricks at the helm. Fortunately, Jan, Rolf's lifelong friend from Amsterdam, and Jan's son Mark, were excellent sailors and they worked hard to keep HO ALOHA moving. Lesa did the cooking and, of course, stood watch as well. Off duty, we snuggled into the forepeak, which at times was like being inside a washing machine, and I felt the baby move. I was convinced it was a girl and thought of the baby as her and she from the beginning. Lesa is tough but she had weak moments worrying about the violent motion and her poor diet. We were distracted from these thoughts and amused watching the moods of our shipmates go up and down like the storm-tossed waves that pitched flat-bottomed HO ALOHA all over the ocean. For a week we listened to World Cup soccer matches on the shortwave radio. When tiny Denmark defeated defending champion Holland in the semifinals our crew, especially Jan and Mark, so cocky and arrogant before the match, were devastated and moped about for days afterwards.

Neptune refused to lighten up, even with the verdant island of Faial in sight. It took us 12 hours of punching and plunging with both engines to knock off the last 36 miles. The marina at Horta never looked better and the first cold Super Bock at Café Sport really hit the spot. That was the only time Lesa complained; she, too, was longing for a cold beer. Jan left us in Horta and fortunately the eight-day passage to Sotogrande, Spain, just around the corner from Gibraltar, was nearly perfect. Steady, favorable winds, sunny skies and daily visits from dolphins and whales accompanied us toward the European continent. I was glad to discover that I hadn't lost my touch at Yahtzee. I defeated Mark and Lesa in a series of tournaments, ranging from the Ho Aloha Championships, to the European Championships, to the World Championships, to the Universe Championships. They stopped playing with me before we reached the Pillars of Hercules.

Lesa and I bid a hasty farewell to HO ALOHA in Sotogrande. We rented a car and made a delightful tour of Andalusia, my favorite part of Spain. From Granada we drove north into the Sierra de Magina, searching for the headwaters of the Guadalquivir River. We followed the often-dry river valley through Andujar, Montoro and Cordoba before arriving in Seville for the World Expo. By the time we returned to Fort Lauderdale Lesa was into her seventh month, our boat was a bit rustier and I was starting to panic. Fatherhood was no longer a grand, romantic notion. It was imminent.

On a rare, singlehanded delivery up the coast to Hilton Head Island, South Carolina, I considered the profound changes looming on my personal horizon. For more than 15 years I had charged off, at a moment's notice, on any sailing adventure that caught my fancy. I had been the master of my fate, the captain of my soul—and all that kind of stuff—and I lived my life with almost complete spontaneity. But now . . . now I was about to become a father. I was scared, scared stiff of the responsibility standing before me like a fenced-in farmyard. I wanted to be a good dad, like my dad, and I was afraid of failure, afraid of my very nature. Thinking about the little life being nourished inside of the woman I so dearly loved brought tears to my eyes. A dark squall was getting darker ahead; I needed to shorten sail. Effortlessly, I slapped in a reef in the main, rolled in a bit of headsail and secured any loose items on deck. The squall came and went, I didn't lose any time or ground and was soon under full sail again.

A modest Gulf Stream squall, that's all it was, one of hundreds I'd weathered before, and will again. But that was the point. I knew all about Gulf Stream squalls but my baby didn't. I knew all about crossing oceans. I knew all about the stars overhead and sea lights or phosphorescence in the water below. I knew all about different countries and cultures. I knew a lot about boats. I knew a lot about mermaids. I knew a lot about myself. There was so much to share with my little baby. It was all so clear, as clear as it had been in the closet those many years ago. I would show my family the world aboard my rusty steel boat. I'd been preparing this chapter in my life for 20 years.

I returned home to a couple of big surprises. A monster hurricane that had seemed to be heading out to sea made an abrupt left turn and was drawing a bead on the Miami-Fort Lauderdale stretch of coastline. Andrew, yes, Andrew, another male storm, was a Category 5 hurricane and although it veered south at the last moment, it shattered the veneer of the South Florida community with 180-mph winds. Andrew struck on Lesa's 30th birthday. As we secured FORTUNA to the dock before heading to my sister's house in the suburbs to ride out the storm, Lesa casually told me that she wanted to have the baby at home.

"What?" I said, hoping I had not heard her correctly.

"I want to have the baby at home. I have a meeting with a midwife next week, what do you think?"

Lesa had not found an obstetrician that she liked, or was at least comfortable with, and she resented their medical approach to pregnancy.

"Being pregnant is not being sick," she told me, and then added, "Did you know that Broward County has one of the highest C-section rates in the country?"

I confessed I didn't know that. Still, the idea of having the baby in our small apartment was terrifying. I had always thought that if and when I had children I would be one of those waiting-room dads with a pocketful of cigars. I had reconciled myself to the fact that I had to be in attendance at the birth but it had never crossed my mind that the birth of my child would not take place in a hospital. Now Lesa was telling me that she was going to have the baby in my own bed and that I was going to help with the delivery!

Driving through Andrew's debris, we met with midwives Adeana Andreau and Sharon Hamilton. After two hours of laughing, chatting and getting to know each other and finding out what was involved in having a home birth, Lesa and I knew that we were doing the right thing. We prepared the apartment and assured nervous relatives that we had a backup doctor on standby and that if there were any complications, we would dash to the hospital. Then we waited. Lesa's due date came and went, no contractions, no baby. Sharon suggested Mexican food; it didn't work. Finally, five days late, Lesa decided to help me work on FORTUNA. I helped her aboard and we spent a few hours dreaming of future voyages. Then, propped on the dock, she vigorously chipped the paint off the old windlass. The next morning she went into labor. Later that day the phone rang. It was Joe.

"Hey, John, I have a delivery for you, a nice boat this time. It's in the Bahamas. Can you go fetch it?"

"Not today, Joe, sorry. I have another delivery to worry about."

"What kind of boat? Where are you going?"

"Actually, Joe, it's a home delivery."

Other books of interest from Sheridan House

CARIBBEAN CRUISING:
YOUR GUIDE TO THE PERFECT SAILING HOLIDAY
by Jane Gibb with John Kretschmer
Expert advice on ideal cruising locations, choosing the best boat,
weather forecasts, equipment, clothes, supplies, expenses, communications,
power needs, health, legal formalities, and much more.

READY FOR SEA!
by Tor Pinney
"...an easy read, packed with good advice. Even experienced cruisers will
pick up a thing or two from this one." *Latitudes & Attitudes*
"...presents clearly and concisely what it takes to provision a boat
and sail it confidently..." *SAIL*

THE SAILOR'S WEATHER GUIDE, 2ND EDITION
by Jeff Markell
"This is one of the best general works I've found." *Sailing World*
"...clear, easy reading that covers with exceptional clarity a subject
a boater ignores at his peril." *Cruising World*

KITCHEN AFLOAT
by Joy Smith
"...answers just about any question a reader might pose...written with
insight, a generous desire to share expert knowledge, and Joy Smith's
characteristic wit." *Long Island Boating World*
"...readies the galley—and you—for food preparation, handling, and safety." *Offshore*

CHANCE THE TIDE
by Kenneth Mowbray
Provides invaluable information for a winter cruise to the Bahamas,
including choosing the right yacht and equipping it properly.
Features assorted tips to make the trip easier. Before you know it
you'll be navigating your way to a beautiful island paradise.

CHARTERING A BOAT
by Chris Caswell
"...a must for potential charterers...very useful for new cruisers as well."
Caribbean Compass
"...gives you good guidelines on what to look for, and what to
take with you when you go." *Latitudes & Attitudes*

America's Favorite Sailing Books
www.sheridanhouse.com